DIABETIC AIR FR[...]
COOKBOOK

CW00555789

Enjoy Medical-Approved Fried Food With Family And Friends Without Regrets. 1500 Days of Quick And Easy Recipes Which Are Mouthwatering For Others And Healthy For You!

Robert Charlies

Table of contents

Introduction

Diabetes is a condition that arises from two reasons when the pancreas cannot produce Insulin enough for body needs or whenever the Insulin it provides may not be utilized properly by the body. Insulin is a blood sugar-regulating hormone. Hyperglycemia, or high blood sugar, is a typical result of uncontrolled diabetes, causing significant harm to the body's structures, especially blood vessels and nerves over time. Diabetes mellitus is a category of illnesses that influence how the body uses glucose. Glucose is essential to your well-being. The cells that make up the muscles and tissues require a significant supply of glucose. It's the brain's primary power supply, too. The primary issue of diabetes varies based on the type of diabetes. And this can result in excessive sugar in the blood, no matter what kind of diabetes a person has. If there is too much sugar, it can lead to grave health issues. The insulin hormone transfers the sugar into the cells from the blood.

High levels of blood sugar may cause harm to your kidneys, eyes, organs, and nerves.

To understand what is the main reason for diabetes, you should know what the normal route of glucose consumption in the body is.

How Glucose and Insulin Work Together

- The pancreas is an organ situated behind and below the stomach that produces Insulin. It is a hormone that regulates the level of sugar in the blood. Here is a step-by-step production in the bloodstream; insulin comes from the pancreases.
- Then Insulin helps the sugar to go into the body cells.
- Insulin reduces the level of sugar in the blood.
- Now that the level of sugar drops in the blood, it also causes the pancreas to secret less amount of Insulin.

- As blood sugar level drops in the body, it reduces insulin secretion from the pancreas.

Types of Diabetes

A metabolic disorder that induces elevated blood sugar is diabetes mellitus, also known as diabetes. To be processed or used for nutrition, the hormone insulin transfers sugar from the blood in the cells. In diabetes, the body does not contain sufficient Insulin or does not utilize the Insulin it generates efficiently. Your brains, lungs, kidneys, and other organs may be affected by uncontrolled elevated blood sugar levels from diabetes.

There are different types of diabetes:

Type 1 Diabetes

A deficiency of the immune system, or an autoimmune disease, results in Type 1 diabetes, also called insulin-dependent diabetes or juvenile diabetes. In the pancreas, your immune system destroys the insulin-producing cells, killing the body's capacity to create Insulin. It's not clear what causes autoimmune disease and how to treat it effectively.

You have to take Insulin to survive with Type 1 diabetes. As an infant or young adult, several individuals are diagnosed. Only 10% of people with diabetes have type 1 diabetes. Symptoms that the body shows on the onset of type 1 diabetes are polyuria (excessive excretion of urine), polydipsia (extreme thirst), sudden weight loss, constant hunger, fatigue, and vision changes. These changes can occur suddenly.

Type 2 Diabetes

Also known as adult-onset diabetes or non-insulin-dependent diabetes, it is caused by the body's inadequate insulin use. Type 2 diabetes is found in the majority of individuals with diabetes. The symptoms can be identical to those with type 1 diabetes. However, much less marked, as a consequence, when symptoms have already occurred, the condition can be detected after many years of diagnosis.

Type 2 diabetes happens when sugar starts adding up in your blood, and the body becomes resistant to Insulin. Type 2 diabetes is insulin resistance. Which ultimately leads to obesity. This in itself is a collection of different diseases. Older generations were more susceptible, but more and more young generations are now being affected. This is a product of bad health, not enough nutrition, and fitness patterns. Your pancreas avoids utilizing Insulin properly in type 2 diabetes. This creates complications with sugar that has to be taken out of the blood and placing it for energy in the cells. Finally, this will add to the need for insulin treatment.

Earlier stages, such as prediabetes, can be controlled successfully through food, exercise, and dynamic blood sugar control. This will also avoid the overall progression of type 2 diabetes. It is possible to monitor diabetes. In certain situations, if sufficient adjustments to the diet are created; on the contrary, the body will go into remission.

Gestational Diabetes

Hyperglycemia with blood glucose levels over average but below those diabetes levels is diagnosed with gestational diabetes. Gestational diabetes is identified via prenatal tests rather than by signs recorded—high blood sugar, which also occurs during gestation. Hormones produced by the placenta are Insulin-blocking, which is the main cause of this type of diabetes. You can manage gestational diabetes much of the time by food and exercise. Usually, it gets resolved after delivery. During pregnancy, gestational diabetes will raise the risk of complications. It will also increase the likelihood that both mothers and infants may experience type 2 diabetes later in life. This form of diabetes is caused by the placenta's production of insulin-blocking hormones.

What Is Air Frying?

An air fryer is comparable to an oven in how it roasts and bakes. Still, the distinction is that the heating elements are situated only on top and supported by a strong, large fan, which results in very crisp food in no time. The air fryer uses spinning-heated air to easily and uniformly cook food instead of using a pot of hot oil. To encourage the hot air to flow evenly around the meal, the meal is put in a metal basket (mesh) or a rack, producing the same light golden, crispy crunch you get from frying in oil. It is easy to use air fryers. Besides, they cook food faster than frying and clean up quickly. You can prepare a selection of healthy foods such as fruits, beef, seafood, poultry, and more, besides making beneficial variants of your favorite fried foods such as chips, onion rings, or French fries.

The air fryer is the modern kitchen tool that is proving its worth in effectively reducing the risk of diabetes, weight loss, and living a healthier life without compromising on fried, fatty, and high-calorie food.

How it Works

The air fryer is a convective heat oven with a revved-up countertop. Its small room enables cooking much quicker. A heating device and a fan are kept at the top of the device. Hot air flows through and around food put in a basket-type fryer. This fast circulation, just like deep frying, renders the food crisp. It's also super quick to clean up, and most systems include dishwasher-safe components.

Benefits Of Using An Air Fryer With Healthier Frying

Once you understand how an air fryer works, you can use it to heat frozen items or cook all types of fresh things like poultry, salmon, other fish, pork chops, and veggies. Most meats do not require additional oil because they are still moist.Season them with salt and your type of herbs and spices, being sure to use dry seasonings because less moisture adds to crispier results.Whether you prefer to baste the steak with any sauce or barbecue sauce, wait until the last few minutes of cooking.

Browning and crisping lean meat pieces, or products with little or no fat, requires a spray of oil. Clean the pork chops and boneless chicken breasts before frying and spritz with a little oil. Vegetable oil or canola oil is preferred because of its higher smoke point, which ensures that it can withstand the severe heat of an air fryer. Vegetables are frequently coated with oil before being air-fried. Season with salt and pepper. Use a less amount than you normally would. The crunchy portions that have been air-fried provide a lot of taste. Fried baby potato halves, broccoli florets, and Brussels sprouts are all delicious. They're incredibly sharp. Sweet potatoes, butternut squash, peppers, and green beans are all sweeter when cooked for a short time.

Benefits of Using Air Fryer

1. **Reduction of Diabetes and Cholesterol Thanks to Less Greasy and Lighter Frying:** Air fryers are popular kitchen appliances used by people who want to cook healthier without sacrificing taste. Air fryers use lower temperatures than other methods of frying to leave food crispier and drier. They also help reduce levels of harmful cholesterol, which can be damaging to the heart health. Air fryers have proven to be an effective way for people with diabetes or high cholesterol levels because they can stay on a low-calorie diet without sacrificing flavor - which is great for those looking for weight loss!
2. **Easy preparation of frozen food:** Another benefit of using an air fryer is that it enables you to prepare frozen food. Frozen potatoes, chicken breasts, and other frozen foods cooked in an air fryer can be reheated to perfect eating (along with vegetables still frozen) by putting them in the oven for just a few minutes.

3. **Healthier Frying:** Air fryers are healthier than high-saturated fat oil because they use lower temperatures while cooking that allows for healthier fats - while also saving time and money while cooking.

Other benefits
- Cleanup is simple.
- Meals that are low in fat
- There is a reduction in the amount of oil required.
- Hot air evenly cooks food.
- Loss of weight Cancer risk is reduced
- Management of diabetes Enhanced memory

According to this food pyramid, you must consume a large portion of healthy vegetables and whole-grain starches, a balanced amount of healthy fats, and proteins with small amounts of nuts and oils.

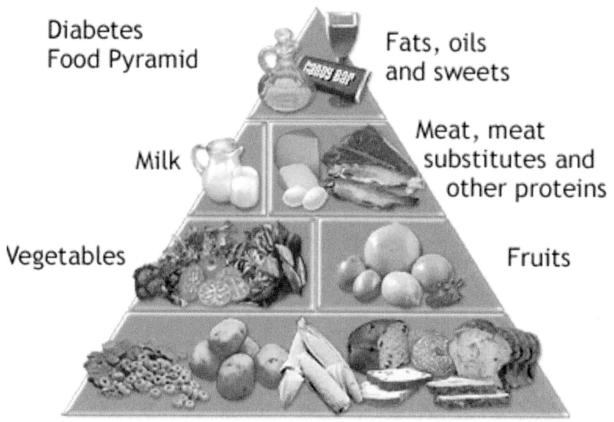

Diabetes
Food Pyramid

Fats, oils
and sweets

Milk

Meat, meat
substitutes and
other proteins

Vegetables

Fruits

Breads, grains and other starches

Healthy Living & Healthy Eating Habits

It is vital to employ the proper combination of several nutrients to achieve optimal health advantages. In general, a healthy diet consists of items from the following categories:

- Smaller quantities of starchy meals including potatoes, bread, pasta, and rice
- Large servings of fruits and vegetables
- Dairy and milk items in small amounts.
- Meat, fish, and eggs are examples of protein foods.
- Non-dairy protein sources include beans, nuts, lentils, and tofu.
- Fatty and sugary foods make up the fifth food group you ingest. However, sugary and fatty foods should only make up a small part of your diet.
- Salmon, sardines, and pilchards must be consumed.
- Dark green vegetables such as broccoli and kale must be consumed
- Calcium-fortified foods, such as fruit juices and soy products.
- Vitamin D helps the body assimilate calcium, so aim to get enough vitamin D from the sun and include vitamin D-rich foods in your diet, such as fortified cereal and fatty fish.
- Substitute polyunsaturated fat for saturated fat as necessary.
- eat at least five servings of vegetables and fruits each day • eat at least two portions of fish per week (ideally fatty fish).
- Begin eating whole grains and nuts daily.
- Limit your salt intake to a little amount per day, such as 6g.
- Alcohol usage has been restricted.

In your diet, limit or avoid the following:

- Commercially manufactured or processed meats, as well as ready-to-eat items high in trans fatty acids and salt.
- Sweetened sugary beverages; refined grains, such as dried cereals or white bread; high-calorie but nutritionally deficient foods, such as cookies, sweets, and crisps

You need the stamina to be active during the day, and the nutrients you need to grow and replenish help you stay balanced and robust, as well as prevent diet-related disorders like diabetes and cancer. Staying busy and eating a good, nutritious diet can also help you maintain a healthier weight.

Some important nutrients, such as vitamins C, A, B, and E, as well as selenium, zinc, and iron, can cause immune system malfunction. By maintaining a healthy weight and eating a nutritious diet low in saturated fat and high in fiber found in whole grains, you can lower your risk of developing type 2 diabetes, improve your heart health, and strengthen your teeth and bones. Eating a well-balanced diet in the right amounts, together with regular exercise, can help you lose weight, lower cholesterol and blood pressure, and minimize your risk of type 2 diabetes.

The following is an example of what your blood glucose level should look like:

Mg/DL	Fasting	After Eating	2-3 hours After Eating
Normal	80-100	170-200	120-140
Impaired Glucose	101-125	190-230	140-160
Diabetic	126 +	220-300	200 +

CHAPTER 1:
Breakfast

1. Ham and Cheese English Muffin Melt

Preparation Time: 10 min   **Cooking Time:** 5 min   **Servings:** 2

Ingredients:

- 1 whole-grain English muffin, split and toasted
- 2 tsp. Dijon mustard
- 2 slices tomato
- 4 thin slices deli ham
- ½ cup shredded Cheddar cheese
- 2 large eggs, fried (optional)

Directions:

1. Preheat the oven broiler on high.
2. Spread each toasted English muffin half with 1 tsp. of mustard and place them on a rimmed baking sheet, cut-side up.
3. Top each with a tomato slice and 2 slices of ham. Sprinkle each with half of the cheese.
4. Broil in the warmed oven until the cheese melts, 2 to 3 minutes.
5. Serve immediately, topped with a fried egg, if desired.

Nutrition Calories: 234 Total Fat: 13 g Saturated Fat: 7 g Sodium: 834 mg Carbohydrates: 16 g Fiber: 3 g Protein: 16g

2.Pumpkin Pie French Toast

Preparation Time: 10 min   **Cooking Time:** 20 min   **Servings:** 4

Ingredients:

- 2 larges, beaten eggs
- 4 slices cinnamon swirl bread
- ¼ cup milk
- ¼ cup pumpkin puree
- ¼ tsp. pumpkin spices
- ¼ cup butter

Directions:

1. In a large mixing bowl, mix milk, eggs, pumpkin puree, and pie spice.
2. Whisk until the mixture is smooth. In the egg mixture, dip the bread on both sides.
3. Place the rack inside of the air fryer's cooking basket.
4. Place 2 slices of bread onto the rack. Set the temperature to 340°F for 10 minutes.
5. Serve pumpkin pie toast with butter.

Nutrition: Calories: 212 Total Fat: 8.2 g Carbs: 7 g Protein: 11.3 g

3. Breakfast Cheese Bread Cups

Preparation Time: 10 min   **Cooking Time:** 15 min   **Servings:** 2

Ingredients:

- 2 eggs
- 2 tbsp. cheddar cheese, grated
- Salt and pepper, to taste
- 1 ham slice, cut into 2 pieces
- 4 bread slices, flatten with a rolling pin

Directions:

1. Spray the inside of 2 ramekins with cooking spray.
2. Place 2 flat pieces of bread into each ramekin. Add the ham slice pieces into each ramekin.
3. Crack an egg in each ramekin, then sprinkle with cheese. Season with salt and pepper.
4. Place the ramekins into the air fryer at 300°F for 15 minutes.
5. Serve warm.

Nutrition: Calories: 162 Total Fat: 8 g Carbs: 10 g Protein: 11 g

4. Crispy Breakfast Avocado Fries

Preparation Time: 10 min   **Cooking Time:** 8 minu   **Servings:** 2

Ingredients:

- 2 eggs, beaten
- 2 large avocados, peeled, pitted, cut into 8 slices each
- ¼ tsp. pepper
- ½ tsp. cayenne pepper
- Salt, to taste
- ½ a lemon, Juice
- ½ cup whole-wheat flour
- 1 cup whole-wheat breadcrumbs
- Greek yogurt to serve

Directions:

1. Add flour, salt, pepper, and cayenne pepper to bowl and mix. Add bread crumbs into another bowl. Beat eggs in a third bowl.
2. First, dredge the avocado slices in the flour mixture.
3. Next, dip them into the egg mixture, and finally dredge them in the breadcrumbs.
4. Place avocado fries into the air fryer basket.
5. Preheat the air fryer to 390°F.
6. Place the air fryer basket into the air fryer and cook for 6 minutes.
7. When cook time is completed, transfer the avocado fries onto a serving platter.
8. Sprinkle with lemon juice and serve with Greek yogurt.

Nutrition: Calories: 272 Total Fat: 13.4 g Carbs: 11.2 g Protein: 15.4 g

5. Cheese and Egg Breakfast Sandwich

Preparation Time: 10 min   **Cooking Time:** 6 min   **Servings:** 1

Ingredients:
- 1–2 eggs
- 1–2 slices cheddar or Swiss cheese
- A bit butters
- 1 roll sliced in half (your choice, Kaiser Bun, English muffin, etc.)

Directions:
1. Butter your sliced roll on both sides.
2. Place the eggs in an oven-safe dish and whisk. Add seasoning if you wish, such as dill, chives, oregano, and salt.
3. Place the egg dish, roll, and cheese into the air fryer.
4. Make assured the buttered sides of the roll are in front of upwards. Set the air fryer to 390°F with a cook time of 6 minutes.
5. Remove the ingredients when cook time is completed by the air fryer.
6. Place the egg and cheese between the pieces of roll and serve warm.
7. You might like to try adding slices of avocado and tomatoes to this breakfast sandwich!

Nutrition: Calories: 212 Total Fat: 11.2 g Carbs: 9.3 g Protein: 12.4 g

6. Peanut Butter and Banana Breakfast Sandwich

Preparation Time: 10 min   **Cooking Time:** 6 min   **Servings:** 1

Ingredients:
- 2 slices whole-wheat bread
- 1 tsp. sugar-free maple syrup
- 1 sliced banana
- 2 tbsp. peanut butter

Directions:
1. Evenly coat both sides of the slices of bread with peanut butter.
2. Add the sliced banana and drizzle with some sugar-free maple syrup.
3. Heat in the air fryer to 330°F for 6 minutes.
4. Serve warm.

Nutrition: Calories: 211 Total Fat: 8.2 g Carbs: 6.3 g Protein: 11.2 g

7. Avocado and Blueberry Muffins

Preparation Time: 10 min   **Cooking Time:** 15 min   **Servings:** 12

Ingredients:

- 2 eggs
- 1 cup blueberries
- 2 cups almond flour
- 1 tsp. baking soda
- ⅛ tsp. salt

For the streusel topping:

- 2 tbsp. Truvia sweetener
- 4 tbsp. butter, softened

- 2 ripe avocados, peeled, pitted, mashed
- 2 tbsp. liquid Stevia
- 1 cup plain Greek yogurt
- 1 tsp. vanilla extract

- 4 tbsp. almond flour

Directions:

1. Make the streusel topping by mixing Truvia, flour, and butter until you form a crumbly mixture. Place this mixture in the freezer for a while.
2. Meanwhile, make the muffins by sifting together flour, baking powder, baking soda, and salt, and set aside. Add avocados and liquid Stevia to a bowl and mix well. Adding in one egg at a time, continue to beat. Add the vanilla extract and yogurt and beat again.
3. Add in flour mixture a bit at a time and mix well. Add the blueberries into the mixture and gently fold them in. Pour the batter into greased muffin cups, then add the mixture until they are half-full.
4. Sprinkle the streusel topping mixture on top of the muffin mixture and place muffin cups in the air fryer basket.
5. Bake in the preheated air fryer at 355°F for 10 minutes. Remove the muffin cups from the air fryer and allow them to cool. Cool completely, then serve.

Nutrition: Calories: 202 Total Fat: 9.2 g Carbs: 7.2 g Protein: 6.3 g

8. Grilled Cheese Sandwiches

Preparation Time: 2 min   **Cooking Time:** 10 min   **Servings:** 2

Ingredients:
- 4 slices American cheese
- 4 slices sandwich bread
- Pat Butter

Directions:
1. Warm your air fryer to 360°F.
2. Fill the center of 2 bread slices with two slices of American cheese.
3. Binge an even layer of butter on each side of the sandwich and position it in the hamper of your air fryer in a single layer.
4. Insert toothpicks on the corners of each sandwich to seal.
5. Air-fries the sandwiches for 4 minutes, flipping once, and cook for another 3 to 4 minutes until toasted.
6. Serve!

Nutrition: Calories: 297 Fat: 14.6 g (7.5 g saturated fat) Cholesterol: 39 mg Sodium: 832 mg Carbohydrates: 31.3 g Dietary Fiber: 1 g Total sugars: 7.1 g Protein: 11.8 g.

9. Air Fryer Bacon

Preparation Time: 2 min   **Cooking Time:** 10 min   **Servings:** 5

Ingredients:
- 5 slices (thick-cut) bacon

Directions:
1. Lay the bacon slices into your air fryer basket, at least 1 inch apart, to cook.
2. Heat the air fryer at 390°F.
3. Cook the bacon for 10 to 12 minutes until crispy.
4. Drain on a kitchen napkin before serving.
5. Enjoy!

Nutrition: Calories: 103 Fat: g (2.6 g saturated fat) Cholesterol: 21 mg Sodium: 439 mg Carbohydrate: 0.3 g Dietary Fiber: 0 g Total Sugars: 0 g Protein: 7 g.

10. Mushroom and Cheese Frittata

Preparation Time: 20 min   **Cooking Time:** 10 min   **Servings:** 4

Ingredients:
- 6 eggs
- 6 cups button mushrooms, sliced thinly
- 1 red onion, sliced into thin rounds
- 6 tbsp. Feta cheese, reduced fat, crumbled
- Pinch salt
- 2 tbsp. olive oil

Directions:
1. Preheat Air Fryer to 330°F.
2. Sauté onions and mushrooms. Transfer to a plate with a paper towel.
3. Meanwhile, beat the eggs in a bowl.
4. Season with salt. Coat a baking dish with cooking spray. Pour egg mixture.
5. Add in mushrooms and onions. Top with crumbled feta cheese.
6. Place baking dish in the Air fryer basket. Cook for 20 minutes. Serve.

Nutrition: Calorie: 140 Carbohydrate: 5.4 g Fat: 10.6 g Protein: 22.7 g Fiber: 1.2 g

11. Air Fried Eggs

Preparation Time: 15 min   **Cooking Time:** 10 min   **Servings:** 4

Ingredients:
- 4 eggs
- 2 cups baby spinach, rinsed
- 1 tbsp. extra-virgin olive oil
- ½ cup cheddar cheese, reduced-fat, shredded, divided
- Bacon, sliced
- Pinch salt
- Pinch pepper

Directions:
1. Preheat the Air Fryer to 350°F.
2. Warm oil in a pan over medium-high flame. Cook the spinach until wilted. Drain the excess liquid. Put the cooked spinach into four greased ramekins.
3. Add a slice of bacon to each ramekin, crack an egg, and put cheese on top.
4. Season with salt and pepper.
5. Put the ramekins inside the cooking basket of the Air Fryer.
6. Cook for 15 minutes.

Nutrition: Calorie: 106 Carbohydrate: 10 g Fat: 3.2 g Protein: 9.0 g Fiber: 1.2 g

CHAPTER 2:
Lunch & Dinner

12. Parmesan Beef Slices

Preparation Time: 14 min   **Cooking Time:** 25 min   **Servings:** 4

Ingredients:
- 12 oz. beef brisket
- 1 tsp. kosher salt
- 7 oz. Parmesan, sliced
- 5 oz. chive stems
- 1 tsp. turmeric
- 1 tsp. dried oregano
- 2 tsp. butter

Directions:
1. Slice the beef brisket into 4 slices.
2. Sprinkle every beef slice with turmeric and dried oregano.
3. Grease the air fryer basket tray with butter.
4. Put the beef slices inside.
5. Dice the chives.
6. Make a layer using the diced chives over the beef slices.
7. Then make a layer using the Parmesan cheese.
8. Preheat the air fryer to 365°F.
9. Cook the beef slices for 25 minutes.

Nutrition: calories 348, fat 18, fiber 0.9, carbs 5, protein 42.1

13. Spinach Beef Heart

Preparation Time: 15 min   **Cooking Time:** 20 min   **Servings:** 4

Ingredients:

- 1-lb. beef heart
- 5 oz. chive stems
- ½ cup fresh spinach
- 1 tsp. salt
- 1 tsp. ground black pepper
- 3 cups chicken stock
- 1 tsp. butter

Directions:

1. Remove all the fat from the beef heart.
2. Dice the chives.
3. Chop the fresh spinach.
4. Combine the diced chives, fresh spinach, and butter together. Stir it.
5. Cut the beef heart and fill it with the spinach-chives mixture.
6. Preheat the air fryer to 400°F.
7. Pour the chicken stock into the air fryer basket tray.
8. Sprinkle the Prepared stuffed beef heart with salt and ground black pepper.
9. Put the beef heart in the air fryer and cook it for 20 minutes.
10. Remove the cooked heart from the air fryer and slice it.
11. Sprinkle the slices with the remaining liquid from the air fryer.

Nutrition: calories 216, fat 6.8, fiber 0.8, carbs 3.8, protein 33.3

14. Chicken Coconut Poppers

Preparation Time: 10 min   **Cooking Time:** 10 min   **Servings:** 6

Ingredients:

- ½ cup coconut flour
- 1 tsp. chili flakes
- 1 tsp. ground black pepper
- 1 tsp. garlic powder
- 11 oz. chicken breast, boneless, skinless
- 1 tbsp. olive oil

Directions:

1. Cut the chicken breast into medium cubes and put them in a large bowl.
2. Sprinkle the chicken cubes with chili flakes, ground black pepper, garlic powder, and stir them well using your hands.
3. After this, sprinkle the chicken cubes with almond flour.
4. Shake the bowl with the chicken cubes gently to coat the meat.
5. Preheat the air fryer to 365°F.
6. Grease the air fryer basket tray with olive oil.
7. Place the chicken cubes inside.
8. Cook the chicken poppers for 10 minutes.
9. Turn the chicken poppers over after 5 minutes of cooking.
10. Allow the cooked chicken poppers to cool before serving.

Nutrition: calories 123, fat 4.6, fiber 3.9, carbs 6.9, protein 13.2

15. Paprika Pulled Pork

Preparation Time: 15 min   **Cooking Time:** 20 min   **Servings:** 4

Ingredients:

- 1 tbsp. chili flakes
- 1 tsp. ground black pepper
- ½ tsp. paprika
- 1 tsp. cayenne pepper
- ⅓ cup cream
- 1 tsp. kosher salt
- 1-lb. pork tenderloin
- 1 tsp. ground thyme
- 4 cup chicken stock
- 1 tsp. butter

Directions:

1. Pour the chicken stock into the air fryer basket tray.
2. Add the pork steak and sprinkle the mixture with chili flakes, ground black pepper, paprika, cayenne pepper, and kosher salt.
3. Preheat the air fryer to 370°F and cook the meat for 20 minutes.
4. Strain the liquid and shred the meat with 2 forks.
5. Then add the butter and cream and mix it.
6. Cook the pulled pork for 4 minutes more at 360°F.
7. When the pulled pork is cooked allow to rest briefly.

Nutrition: calories 198, fat 6.8, fiber 0.5, carbs 2.3, protein 30.7

16. Cheddar Chicken Drumsticks

Preparation Time: 18 min   **Cooking Time:** 13 min   **Servings:** 4

Ingredients:

- 1-lb. chicken drumstick
- 6 oz. Cheddar cheese, sliced
- 1 tsp. dried rosemary
- 1 tsp. dried oregano
- ½ tsp. salt
- ½ tsp. chili flakes

Directions:

1. Sprinkle the chicken drumsticks with dried rosemary, dried oregano, salt, and chili flakes.
2. Massage the drumsticks carefully and leave for 5 minutes to marinade.
3. Preheat the air fryer to 370°F.
4. Place the marinated chicken drumsticks in the air fryer tray and cook them for 10 minutes.
5. Turn the chicken drumsticks over and cover them with a layer of sliced cheese.
6. Cook the chicken for 3 minutes more at the same temperature.
7. Then transfer the chicken drumsticks onto a large serving plate.
8. Serve the dish hot – the cheese should be melted.

Nutrition: calories 226, fat 9.8, fiber 0.3, carbs 1, protein 16.4

17. Garlic Beef Steak

Preparation Time: 15 min   **Cooking Time:** 12 minu   **Servings:** 4

Ingredients:

- 1 tbsp. butter
- 2 tbsp. fresh orange juice
- 1 tsp. lime zest
- 1-lb. beef steak
- 1 tsp. ground ginger
- 1 tsp. dried oregano
- 1 tbsp. cream
- ½ tsp. minced garlic

Directions:

1. Combine the fresh orange juice, butter, lime zest, ground ginger, dried oregano, cream, and minced garlic together.
2. Combine the mixture well.
3. Then tenderize the steak gently.
4. Brush the beefsteak with the combined spice, mix carefully and leave the steak for 7 minutes to marinade.
5. Preheat the air fryer to 360°F.
6. Put the marinated beef steak in the air fryer basket and cook the meat for 12 minutes. The beef should be well done.

Nutrition: calories 245, fat 10.2, fiber 0.3, carbs 1.7, protein 34.6

18. Air Fryer Pork Ribs

Preparation Time: 30 min   **Cooking Time:** 30 min   **Servings:** 5

Ingredients:

- 1 tbsp. apple cider vinegar
- 1 tsp. cayenne pepper
- 1 tsp. minced garlic
- 1 tsp. mustard
- 1 tsp. chili flakes
- 16 oz. pork ribs
- 1 tsp. sesame oil
- 1 tsp. salt
- 1 tbsp. paprika

Directions:

1. Sprinkle the pork ribs with cayenne pepper, apple cider vinegar, minced garlic, mustard, and chili flakes.
2. Add the sesame oil and salt.
3. Add paprika and mix it into the pork ribs carefully.
4. Leave the ribs in the fridge for 20 minutes.
5. Preheat the air fryer to 360°F.
6. Transfer the pork ribs to the air fryer basket and cook them for 15 minutes.
7. Turn the pork ribs over and cook the meat for 15 minutes more.

Nutrition: calories 265, fat 17.4, fiber 0.7, carbs 1.4, protein 24.5 144 mg

19. Bagel Crust Fish Fillets

Preparation Time: 10 min   **Cooking Time:** 10 min   **Servings:** 4

Ingredients:

- 4 white fish fillets
- 1 tbsp. mayonnaise
- 1 tsp. lemon-pepper seasoning
- 2 tbsp. almond flour
- ¼ cup bagel seasoning

Directions:

1. In a small bowl, mix together bagel seasoning, almond flour, and lemon pepper seasoning.
2. Brush mayonnaise over fish fillets. Sprinkle seasoning mixture over fish fillets.
3. Place the cooking tray in the air fryer basket. Line air fryer basket with parchment paper.
4. Select Bake mode.
5. Set time to 10 minutes and temperature 400°F then press START.
6. The air fryer display will prompt you to ADD FOOD once the temperature is reached then place fish fillets in the air fryer basket.
7. Serve and enjoy.

Nutrition: Calories 375 Fat 2.5 g Carbohydrates 7.2 g Sugar 1 g Protein 41.3 g Cholesterol 120 mgj

20. Easy Air Fryer Scallops

Preparation Time: 10 min   **Cooking Time:** 4 min   **Servings:** 2

Ingredients:

- 8 scallops
- 1 tbsp. olive oil
- Pepper
- Salt

Directions:

1. Brush scallops with olive oil and season with pepper and salt.
2. Place the cooking tray in the air fryer basket.
3. Select Air Fry mode.
4. Set time to 2 minutes and temperature 390°F then press START.
5. The air fryer display will prompt you to ADD FOOD once the temperature is reached then add scallops in the air fryer basket.
6. Turn scallops and air fry for 2 minutes more.
7. Serve and enjoy.

Nutrition: Calories 166 Fat 7.9 g Carbohydrates 2.9 g Sugar 0 g Protein 20.2 g Cholesterol 40 mg

21. Moist & Juicy Baked Cod

Preparation Time: 10 min   **Cooking Time:** 10 min   **Servings:** 2

Ingredients:

- 1 lb. cod fillets
- 1 ½ tbsp. olive oil
- 3 dashes cayenne pepper
- 1 tbsp. lemon juice
- ¼ tsp. salt

Directions:

1. In a small bowl, mix together olive oil, cayenne pepper, lemon juice, and salt.
2. Brush fish fillets with oil mixture.
3. Place the cooking tray in the air fryer basket. Line air fryer basket with parchment paper.
4. Select Bake mode.
5. Set time to 10 minutes and temperature 400 F then press START.
6. The air fryer display will prompt you to ADD FOOD once the temperature is reached then place fish fillets in the air fryer basket.
7. Serve and enjoy.

Nutrition: Calories 275 Fat 12.7 g Carbohydrates 0.4 g Sugar 0.2 g Protein 40.6 g Cholesterol 111 mg

22. Scrambled Eggs

Preparation Time: 5 min   **Cooking Time:** 20 min   **Servings:** 2

Ingredients:

- 4 large eggs.
- ½ cup shredded sharp Cheddar cheese.
- 2 tbsp. unsalted butter; melted.

Directions:

1. Crack eggs into a 2-cup round baking dish and whisk.
2. Place dish into the air fryer basket.
3. Adjust the temperature to 400 Degrees F and set the timer for 10 minutes.
4. After 5 minutes, stir the eggs and add the butter and cheese.
5. Let cook for 3 more minutes and stir again.
6. Allow eggs to finish cooking an additional 2 minutes or remove if they are to your desired liking.
7. Use a fork to fluff. Serve warm.

Nutrition: Calories: 359 Protein: 19.5g Fiber: 0.0g Fat: 27.6g Carbs: 1.1g

23. Beef-Chicken Meatball Casserole

Preparation Time: 15 min   **Cooking Time:** 21 min   **Servings:** 7

Ingredients:

- 1 eggplant
- 10 oz. ground chicken
- 8 oz. ground beef
- 1 tsp. minced garlic
- 1 tsp. ground white pepper
- 1 tomato
- 1 egg
- 1 tbsp. coconut flour
- 8 oz. Parmesan, shredded
- 2 tbsp. butter
- ⅓ cup cream

Directions:

1. Combine the ground chicken and ground beef in a large bowl.
2. Add the minced garlic and ground white pepper.
3. Crack the egg into the bowl with the ground meat mixture and stir it carefully until well combined.
4. Then add the coconut flour and mix.
5. Make small meatballs from the ground meat.
6. Preheat the air fryer to 360°F.
7. Sprinkle the air fryer basket tray with the butter and pour the cream.
8. Peel the eggplant and chop it.
9. Put the meatballs over the cream and sprinkle them with the chopped eggplant.
10. Slice the tomato and place it over the eggplant.
11. Make a layer of shredded cheese over the sliced tomato.
12. Put the casserole in the air fryer and cook it for 21 minutes.
13. Let the casserole cool to room temperature before serving.

Nutrition: calories 314, fat 16.8, fiber 3.4, carbs 7.5, protein 33.9

CHAPTER 3:

Snack & Appetizer

---

24. Crispy Eggplant Fries

Preparation Time: 7 min   **Cooking Time:** 12 min   **Servings:** 3

Ingredients:

- 2 eggplants
- ¼ cup olive oil
- ¼ cup almond flour
- ½ cup water

Directions:

1. Preheat your air fryer to 390°F. Cut the eggplants into ½-inch slices. In a mixing bowl, mix the flour, olive oil, water, and eggplants.

2. Slowly coat the eggplants. Add eggplants to the air fryer and cook for 12 minutes. Serve with yogurt or tomato sauce.

Nutrition: Calories: 103 Total Fat: 7.3 g Carbs: 12.3 g Protein: 1.9 g

---

25. Charred Bell Peppers

Preparation Time: 7 min   **Servings:** 3

Cooking Time: 4 min

Ingredients:

- 20 bell peppers, sliced and seeded
- 1 tsp. olive oil
- 1 pinch sea salt
- 1 lemon
- Pepper

Directions:

1. Preheat your air fryer to 390°F. Sprinkle the peppers with oil and salt. Cook the peppers in the air fryer for 4 minutes.

2. Place peppers in a large bowl, and squeeze lemon juice over the top. Season with salt and pepper.

Nutrition: Calories: 30 Total Fat: 0.25 g Carbs: 6.91 g Protein: 1.28 g

26. Cheese & Onion Nuggets

Preparation Time: 7 min   **Cooking Time:** 12 min   **Servings:** 4

Ingredients:
- 7 oz. Edam cheese, grated
- 2 spring onions, diced
- 1 egg, beaten
- 1 tbsp. coconut oil
- 1 tbsp. thyme, dried
- Salt and pepper to taste

Directions:
1. Mix the onion, cheese, coconut oil, salt, pepper, thyme in a bowl. Make 8 small balls and place the cheese in the center.
2. Place in the fridge for about an hour. With a pastry brush, carefully brush the beaten egg over the nuggets. Cook for 12 minutes in the air fryer at 350°F.

Nutrition: Calories:227 Total Fat:17.3 g Carbs:4.5 g Protein:14.2 g

27. Keto French fries

Preparation Time: 7 min   **Cooking Time:** 20 min   **Servings:** 4

Ingredients:
- 1 large rutabaga, peeled, cut into spears about ¼-inch wide
- Salt and pepper to taste
- ½ tsp. paprika
- 2 tbsp. coconut oil

Directions:
1. Preheat your air fryer to 450°F. Mix the oil, paprika, salt, and pepper.
2. Pour the oil mixture over the rutabaga fries, making sure all pieces are well coated. Cook in the air fryer for 20 minutes or until crispy.

Nutrition: Calories: 113 Total Fat: 7.2 g Carbs: 12.5 g Protein: 1.9 g

28. Fried Garlic Green Tomatoes

Preparation Time: 7 min   **Cooking Time:** 12 min   **Servings:** 2

Ingredients:

- 3 green tomatoes, sliced
- ½ cup almond flour
- 2 eggs, beaten
- Salt and pepper to taste
- 1 tsp. garlic, minced

Directions:

1. Season the tomatoes with salt, garlic, and pepper. Preheat your air fryer to 400°F. Dip the tomatoes first in flour then in the egg mixture.

2. Spray the tomato rounds with olive oil and place them in the air fryer basket. Cook for 8 minutes, then flip over and cook for additional 4 minutes. Serve with zero-carb mayonnaise.

Nutrition: Calories: 123 Total Fat: 3.9 g Carbs: 16 g Protein: 8.4 g

29. Garlic Cauliflower Tots

Preparation Time: 7 min   **Cooking Time:** 20 min   **Servings:** 4

Ingredients:

- 1 crown cauliflower, chopped in a food processor
- ½ cup parmesan cheese, grated
- Salt and pepper to taste
- ¼ cup almond flour
- 2 eggs
- 1 tsp. garlic, minced

Directions:

1. Mix all the ingredients. Shape into tots and spray with olive oil. Preheat your air fryer to 400°F.

2. Cook for 10 minutes on each side.

Nutrition: Calories: 18 Total Fat: 0.6 g Carbs: 1.3 g Protein: 1.8 g

30. Air Fried Ripe Plantains

Preparation Time: 10 min   **Cooking Time:** 10 min   **Servings:** 2

Ingredients:

- 2 pcs. large ripe plantain, peeled, sliced into inch thick disks
- 1 tbsp. coconut butter, unsweetened

Directions:

1. Preheat the air fryer to 350°F.
2. Brush a small amount of coconut butter on all sides of plantain disks.
3. Place one even layer into the air fryer basket, making sure none overlap or touch. Fry plantains for 10 minutes.
4. Remove from the basket. Place on plates. Repeat step for all plantains.
5. While plantains are still warm. Serve.

Nutrition: Calories: 209 Carbs: 29 g Fat: 8 g Protein: 2.9 g Fiber: 3.5 g

31. Garlic Bread with Cheese Dip

Preparation Time: 10 min   **Cooking Time:** 5 min   **Servings:** 4

Ingredients:

- Fried garlic bread
- 1 medium baguette, halved lengthwise, cut sides toasted
- 2 garlic cloves, whole
- 4 tbsp. extra-virgin olive oil
- 2 tbsp. fresh parsley, minced

Blue cheese dip:

- 1 tbsp. fresh parsley, minced
- ¼ cup fresh chives, minced
- ¼ tsp. Tabasco sauce
- 1 tbsp. lemon juice, freshly squeezed
- ½ cup Greek yogurt, low-fat
- ¼ cup blue cheese, reduced fat
- 1/16 tsp. salt
- 1/16 tsp. white pepper

Directions:

1. Preheat the machine to 400°F.
2. Mix oil and parsley in a small bowl.
3. Vigorously rub garlic cloves on cut/toasted sides of the baguette. Dispose of garlic nubs.
4. Using a pastry brush, spread parsley-infused oil on the cut side of the bread.
5. Place the bread cut-side down on a chopping board. Slice into inch-thick half-moons.
6. Place bread slices in an air fryer basket. Fry for 3 to 5 minutes or until bread browns a little. Shake contents of the basket once midway through. Place cooked pieces on a serving platter. Repeat the step for the remaining bread.
7. To prepare blue cheese dip, mix all the ingredients in a bowl.
8. Place equal portions of fried bread on plates. Serve with blue cheese dip on the side.

Nutrition: Calories: 209 Carbs: 29 g Fat: 8 g Protein: 2.9 g Fiber: 3.5 g

32. Air Fried Plantains in Coconut Sauce

Preparation Time: 10 min   **Cooking Time:** 10 min   **Servings:** 4

Ingredients:

- 6 ripe plantains, peeled, quartered lengthwise
- 1 can coconut cream
- 2 tbsp. of honey
- 1 tbsp. coconut oil

Directions:

1. Preheat the air fryer to 330°F.
2. Pour coconut cream in a thick-bottomed saucepan set over high heat; bring to boil. Reduce heat to lowest setting; simmer uncovered until the cream is reduced by half and darkens in color. Turn off heat.
3. Whisk in honey until smooth. Cool completely before using. Lightly grease a non-stick skillet with coconut oil.
4. Layer plantains in the air fryer basket and fry for 10 minutes or until golden on both sides; drain on paper towels. Place plantain on plates.
5. Drizzle in a small amount of coconut sauce. Serve.

Nutrition: Calories: 236 Carbs: 0 g Fat: 1.5 g Protein: 1 g Fiber: 1.8 g

33. Beef and Mango Skewers

Preparation Time: 10 min   **Cooking Time:** 6 min   **Servings:** 4

Ingredients:

- ¾ lb. (340-g.) of beef sirloin tip, cut into 1-inch cubes
- 2 tbsp. balsamic vinegar
- 1 tbsp. olive oil
- 1 tbsp. honey
- ½ tsp. dried marjoram
- Pinch salt
- Freshly ground black pepper to taste
- 1 mango

Directions:

1. Put the beef cubes in a medium bowl and add the balsamic vinegar, olive oil, honey, marjoram, salt, and pepper. Mix well, then rub the marinade into the beef with your hands. Set aside.
2. To prepare the mango, stand it on end and cut the skin off using a sharp knife. Then carefully cut around the oval pit to remove the flesh. Cut the mango into 1-inch cubes.
3. Thread metal skewers alternating with 3 beef cubes and 2 mango cubes. Place the skewers in the air fryer basket.
4. Air fry at 390°F (199°C) for 4 to 7 minutes or until the beef is browned and at least 145°F (63°C).

Nutrition: Calories: 245 Fat: 9 g Protein: 26 g Carbs: 15 g Fiber: 1 g Sugar: 14 g Sodium: 96 mg

34. Basil Pesto Bruschetta

Preparation Time: 10 min   **Cooking Time:** 6 min   **Servings:** 4

Ingredients:

- 8 slices French bread, ½-inch thick
- 2 tbsp. softened butter
- 1 cup shredded Mozzarella cheese
- ½ cup basil pesto
- 1 cup chopped grape tomatoes
- 2 green onions, thinly sliced

Directions:

1. Spread the bread with the butter and place butter-side up in the air fryer basket. Bake at 350°F (177°C) for 3 to 5 minutes or until the bread is light golden brown.
2. Remove the bread from the basket and top each piece with some of the cheese. Return to the basket in batches and bake until the cheese melts for about 1 to 3 minutes.
3. Meanwhile, combine the pesto, tomatoes, and green onions in a small bowl.
4. When the cheese has melted, remove the bread from the air fryer and place it on a serving plate. Top each slice with some of the pesto mixture and serve.

Nutrition: Calories: 463 Fat: 25 g Protein: 19 g Carbs: 41 g Fiber: 3 g Sugar: 2 g Sodium: 822 mg

CHAPTER 4:

Poultry

---

35. Warm Chicken and Spinach Salad

Preparation Time: 10 min   **Cooking Time:** 18 min   **Servings:** 4

Ingredients:

- 3 (5 oz.) low-sodium boneless, skinless chicken breasts, cut into 1-inch cubes
- 5 tsp. olive oil
- ½ tsp. dried thyme
- 1 medium red onion, sliced
- 1 red bell pepper, sliced
- 1 small zucchini, cut into strips
- 3 tbsp. freshly squeezed lemon juice
- 6 cups fresh baby spinach

Directions:

1. In a huge bowl, blend the chicken with olive oil and thyme. Toss to coat. Transfer to a medium metal bowl and roast for 8 minutes in the air fryer.
2. Add the red onion, red bell pepper, and zucchini. Roast for 8 to 12 more minutes, stirring once during cooking, or until the chicken grasps an inner temperature of 165°F on a meat thermometer.
3. Remove the bowl from the air fryer and stir in the lemon juice.
4. Lay the spinach in a serving bowl and top with the chicken mixture. Toss to combine and serve immediately.

Nutrition: Calories: 214 Fat: 7 g (29% of calories from fat) Saturated Fat: 1 g Protein: 28 g Carbs: 7 g Sodium: 116 mg Fiber: 2 g

36. Italian Whole Chicken

Preparation Time: 10 min   **Cooking Time:** 35 min   **Servings:** 4

Ingredients:

- 1 whole chicken
- 2 tbsp. or oil spray of choice
- 1 tsp. garlic powder
- 1 tsp. onion powder

- 1 tsp. paprika
- 1 tsp. Italian seasoning
- 2 tbsp. Montreal steak seasoning
- 1½ cup chicken broth

Directions:

1. Whisk all the seasonings in a bowl and rub it on the chicken.
2. Set a metal rack in the air fryer oven and pour broth into it.
3. Place the chicken on the metal rack, then put on its pressure-cooking lid.
4. Hit the "Pressure Button" and select 25 minutes of cooking time, then press "Start."
5. Once the air fryer oven beeps, do a natural release and remove its lid.
6. Transfer the pressure-cooked chicken to a plate.
7. Empty the pot and set an air fryer basket in the oven.
8. Toss the chicken pieces with oil to coat well.
9. Spread the seasoned chicken in the air fryer basket.
10. Put on the lid and hit the "Air Fryer Button," then set the time to 10 minutes.
11. Remove the lid and serve.
12. Enjoy!

Nutrition: Calories: 163 Total Fat: 10.7 g Saturated Fat: 2 g Cholesterol: 33 mg Sodium: 1439 mg Total Carbs: 1.8 g Dietary Fiber: 0.3 g Total Sugars: 0.8 g Protein: 12.6 g

37. Ranch Chicken Wings

Preparation Time: 10 min   **Cooking Time:** 35 min   **Servings:** 3

Ingredients:

- 12 chicken wings
- 1 tbsp. olive oil
- 1 cup chicken broth
- ¼ cup butter
- ½ cup red hot sauce
- ¼ tsp. Worcestershire sauce
- 1 tbsp. white vinegar
- ¼ tsp. cayenne pepper
- ⅛ tsp. garlic powder
- Seasoned salt to taste
- Black pepper
- Ranch dressing for dipping
- Celery to garnish

Directions:

1. Set the air fryer basket in the air fryer oven and pour the broth into it.
2. Spread the chicken wings in the basket and put on the pressure-cooking lid.
3. Hit the "Pressure Button" and select 10 minutes of cooking time, then press "Start."
4. Meanwhile, for the sauce preparation, add butter, vinegar, cayenne pepper, garlic powder, Worcestershire sauce, and spicy sauce in a small saucepan.
5. Stir and cook this sauce for 5 minutes on medium heat until it thickens.
6. Once the air fryer oven beeps, do a quick release and remove its lid.
7. Remove the wings and empty the air fryer oven Duo.
8. Toss the wings with oil, salt, and black pepper.
9. Set the air fryer basket in the oven and arrange the wings in it.
10. Put on the lid and seal it.
11. Hit the "Air Fryer Button" and select 20 minutes of cooking time, then press "Start."
12. Once the air fryer oven beeps, remove its lid.
13. Transfer the wings to the sauce and mix well.
14. Serve.

Nutrition: Calories: 414 Total Fat: 31.6 g Saturated Fat: 11 g Cholesterol: 98 mg Sodium: 568 mg Total Carbs: 11.2 g Dietary Fiber: 0.3 g Total Sugars: 0.2 g Protein: 20.4 g

38. Chicken Mac and Cheese

Preparation Time: 10 min **Cooking Time:** 9 min **Servings:** 4

Ingredients:

- 2 ½ cups macaroni
- 2 cups chicken stock
- 1 cup cooked chicken, shredded
- 1 ¼ cup heavy cream
- 8 tbsp. butter
- 1 bag Ritz crackers

Directions:

1. Add chicken stock, heavy cream, chicken, 4 tbsp. butter, and macaroni to the air fryer oven Duo.
2. Put on the pressure-cooking lid and seal it.
3. Hit the "Pressure Button" and select 4 minutes of cooking time, then press "Start."
4. Crush the crackers and mix them well with 4 tbsp. of melted butter.
5. Once the air fryer oven beeps, do a quick release and remove its lid.
6. Put on the lid and seal it.
7. Hit the "Air Fryer Button" and select 5 minutes of cooking time, then press "Start."
8. Once the air fryer oven beeps, remove its lid.
9. Serve.

Nutrition: Calories: 611 Total Fat: 43.6 g Saturated Fat: 26.8 g Cholesterol: 147 mg Sodium: 739 mg Total Carbs: 29.5 g Dietary Fiber: 1.2 g Total Sugars: 1.7 g Protein: 25.4 g

39. Bacon-Wrapped Chicken

Preparation Time: 10 min **Cooking Time:** 24 min **Servings:** 4

Ingredients:

- ¼ cup maple syrup
- 1 tsp. ground black pepper
- 1 tsp. Dijon mustard
- ¼ tsp. garlic powder
- ⅛ tsp. kosher salt
- 4 (6 oz.) skinless, boneless chicken breasts
- 8 slices bacon

Directions:

1. Whisk maple syrup with salt, garlic powder, mustard, and black pepper in a small bowl.
2. Rub the chicken with salt and black pepper, and wrap each chicken breast with 2 slices of bacon.
3. Place the wrapped chicken in the Air fryer oven baking pan.
4. Brush the wrapped chicken with maple syrup mixture.
5. Put on the lid and seal it.
6. Hit the "Bake Button" and select 20 cooking times, then press "Start."
7. Once the function is completed, switch the pot to "Broil" mode and cook for 4 minutes.
8. Serve.

Nutrition: Calories: 441 Total Fat: 18.3 g Saturated Fat: 5.2 g Cholesterol: 141 mg Sodium: 1081 mg Total Carbs: 14 g Dietary Fiber: 0.1 g Total Sugars: 11.8 g Protein: 53.6 g

40. Creamy Chicken Thighs

Preparation Time: 10 min   **Cooking Time:** 30 min   **Servings:** 2

Ingredients:

- 1 tbsp. olive oil
- 6 chicken thighs, bone-in, skin-on
- Salt
- Freshly ground black pepper
- ¾ cup low-sodium chicken broth
- ½ cup heavy cream
- ½ cup sun-dried tomatoes, chopped
- ¼ cup Parmesan, grated
- Freshly torn basil to serve

Directions:

1. Hit the "Sauté Button" on the Air fryer oven and add oil to heat.
2. Stir in chicken, salt, and black pepper, then sear for 5 minutes per side.
3. Add broth, cream, parmesan, and tomatoes.
4. Put on the Air Fryer lid and seal it.
5. Hit the "Bake Button" and select 20 minutes of cooking time, then press "Start."
6. Once the Air Fryer oven beeps, remove its lid.
7. Garnish with basil and serve.

Nutrition: Calories 454 Total Fat 37.8g Saturated Fat 14.4g Cholesterol 169mg Sodium: 181 mg Total Carbs: 2.8 g Dietary Fiber: 0.7 g Total Sugars: 0.7 g Protein: 26.9 g

41. Air Fryer Teriyaki Hen Drumsticks

Preparation Time: 30 min   **Cooking Time:** 20 min   **Servings:** 4

Ingredients:

- 6 poultry drumsticks
- 1 mug teriyaki sauce

Directions:

1. Mix drumsticks with teriyaki sauce in a zip-lock bag. Let the sauce rest for half an hour.
2. Preheat your air fryer to 360°F.
3. Abode the drumsticks in one layer in the air fryer basket and cook for 20 minutes. Shake the basket pair times through food preparation.
4. Garnish with sesame seeds and sliced onions

Nutrition: Calories: 163 Carbs: 7 g Protein: 16 g Fat: 7 g

42. Rolled Turkey Breast

Preparation Time: 5 min   **Cooking Time:** 10 min   **Servings:** 4

Ingredients:

- 1 box cherry tomatoes
- ¼ lb. turkey blanket

Directions:

1. Wrap the turkey and blanket in the tomatoes, close with the help of toothpicks.
2. Take to Air Fryer for 10 minutes at 3900F.
3. You can increase the filling with ricotta and other preferred light ingredients.

Nutrition: Calories: 172 Carbohydrates: 3g Fat: 2g Protein: 34g Sugar: 1g Cholesterol: 300mg

43. Chicken with Lemon and Bahian Seasoning

Preparation Time: 2 hours   **Cooking Time:** 20 min   **Servings:** 4

Ingredients:

- 5 pieces chicken to a bird;
- 2 garlic cloves, crushed;
- 4 tbsp. lemon juice;
- 1 coffee spoon of Bahian spices;
- salt and black pepper to taste.

Directions:

1. Place the chicken pieces in a covered bowl and add the spices. Add the lemon juice. Cover the container and let the chicken marinate for 2 hours.
2. Place each piece of chicken in the basket of the air fryer, without overlapping the pieces. Set the fryer for 20 minutes at 390°F. In half the time, brown evenly. Serve!

Nutrition: Calories: 316.2 Carbohydrates: 4.9g Fat: 15.3g Protein: 32.8g Sugar: 0g

44. Faire-Worthy Turkey Legs

Preparation Time: 5 min   **Cooking Time:** 10 min   **Servings:** 4

Ingredients:
- I turkey leg
- 1 tsp. olive oil
- 1 tsp. poultry seasoning
- 1 tsp. garlic powder
- salt and black pepper to taste

Directions:
1. Warm up the air fryer to 350°F for about 4 minutes.
2. Coat the leg with olive oil. Just use your hands and rub them in.
3. In a small bowl, mix the poultry seasoning, garlic powder, salt, and pepper. Rub it on the turkey leg.
4. Coat the inside of the air fryer basket with nonstick spray and place the turkey leg in.
5. Cook for 27 minutes, turning at 14 minutes. Be sure the leg is done by inserting a meat thermometer in the fleshy part of the leg and it should read 165°F.

Nutrition: Calories: 325 Carbohydrates: 8.3g Fat: 10g Protein: 18g

45. Tasty Hassel back Chicken

Preparation Time: 10 min   **Cooking Time:** 18 min   **Servings:** 2

Ingredients:
- 2 lbs chicken breasts, boneless and skinless
- ½ cup sauerkraut, squeezed and remove excess liquid
- 2 tbsp. thin Swiss cheese slices, tear into pieces
- 1 lbs thin deli corned beef slices, tear into pieces
- Salt and Pepper as per taste

Directions:
1. Make five slits on top of chicken breasts. Season chicken with pepper and salt.
2. Stuff each slit with beef, sauerkraut, and cheese.
3. Spray chicken with cooking spray and place in the air fryer basket.
4. Cook chicken at 350°F for 18 minutes.
5. Serve and enjoy.

Nutrition: Calories 724 Fat 39.9 g Carbohydrates 3.6 g Sugar 2.6 g Protein 83.6 g Cholesterol 260 mg

CHAPTER 5:

Beef

46. Meatloaf Slider Wraps

Preparation Time: 15 min   **Cooking Time:** 10 min   **Servings:** 2

Ingredients:

- 1 lb. ground beef, grass-fed
- ½ cup almond flour
- ¼ cup coconut flour
- ½ tbsp. minced garlic
- ¼ cup chopped white onion
- 1 tsp. Italian seasoning
- ½ tsp. sea salt
- ½ tsp. dried tarragon
- ½ tsp. ground black pepper
- 1 tbsp. Worcestershire sauce
- ¼ cup ketchup
- 2 eggs, pastured, beaten
- 1 head of lettuce

Directions:

1. Place all the ingredients in a bowl, stir well, then shape the mixture into 2-inch diameters and 1-inch-thick patties and refrigerate them for 10 minutes.
2. Meanwhile, switch on the air fryer, insert the fryer basket, grease it with olive oil, then shut with its lid, set the fryer at 360°F, and preheat for 10 minutes.
3. Open the fryer, add patties to it in a single layer, close with its lid and cook for 10 minutes until nicely golden and cooked, flipping the patties halfway through the frying.
4. When the air fryer beeps, open its lid and transfer patties to a plate.
5. Wrap each patty in lettuce and serve.

Nutrition: Calories: 228 Carbs: 6 g Fat: 16 g Protein: 13 g Fiber: 2 g

47. Beef Schnitzel

Preparation Time: 10 min   **Cooking Time:** 15 min   **Servings:** 1

Ingredients:

- 1 lean beef schnitzel
- 2 tbsp. olive oil
- ¼ cup breadcrumbs
- 1 egg
- 1 lemon and salad greens to serve

Directions:

1. Let the air fryer heat to 180°C.
2. In a big bowl, add breadcrumbs and oil, mix well until it forms a crumbly mixture.
3. Dip beef steak in whisked egg and coat in breadcrumbs mixture.
4. Place the breaded beef in the air fryer and cook at 180°C for 15 minutes or more until fully cooked through.
5. Take out from the air fryer and serve with the side of salad greens and lemon.

Nutrition: Calories: 340 Proteins: 20 g Carbs: 14 g Fat: 10 g Fiber: 7 g

48. Steak with Asparagus Bundles

Preparation Time: 20 min   **Cooking Time:** 30 min   **Servings:** 2

Ingredients:

- Olive oil spray
- 2 lb. flank steak, cut into 6 pieces
- Kosher salt and black pepper
- 2 cloves minced garlic
- 4 cups asparagus
- ½ Tamari sauce
- 3 bell peppers sliced thinly
- ⅓ cup beef broth
- 1 tbsp. unsalted butter
- ¼ cup balsamic vinegar

Directions:

1. Sprinkle salt and pepper on steak and rub.
2. In a Ziploc bag, add garlic and Tamari sauce, then add steak, toss well and seal the bag.
3. Let it marinate for 1 hour or overnight.
4. Equally, place bell peppers and asparagus in the center of the steak.
5. Roll the steak around the vegetables and secure well with toothpicks.
6. Preheat the air fryer.
7. Drizzle the steak with olive oil spray. And place steaks in the air fryer.
8. Cook for 15 minutes at 400°F or more until steaks are cooked.
9. Take the steak out from the air fryer and let it rest for 5 minutes.
10. Remove steak bundles and allow them to rest for 5 minutes before serving and slicing.
11. In the meantime, add butter, balsamic vinegar, and broth over medium flame. Mix well and reduce it by half. Add salt and pepper to taste.
12. Pour over steaks right before serving.

Nutrition: Calories: 471 Proteins: 29 g Carbs: 20 g Fat: 15 g

49. Beef Steak Kabobs with Vegetables

Preparation Time: 30 min   **Cooking Time:** 10 min   **Servings:** 4

Ingredients:

- 2 tbsp. light soy sauce
- 4 cups lean beef chuck ribs, cut into 1-inch pieces
- ⅓ cup low-fat sour cream
- ½ onion
- 8 (6-inch) skewers
- 1 bell pepper
- Black pepper
- Yogurt for dipping

Directions:

1. In a mixing bowl, add soy sauce and sour cream, mix well. Add the lean beef chunks, coat well, and let it marinate for half an hour or more.
2. Cut onion, bell pepper into 1-inch pieces. In water, soak skewers for 10 minutes.
3. Add onions, bell peppers, and beef on skewers; alternatively, sprinkle with black pepper.
4. Let it cook for 10 minutes in a preheated air fryer at 400°F, flip halfway through.
5. Serve with yogurt dipping sauce.

Nutrition: Calories: 268 Proteins: 20 g Carbs: 15 g Fat: 10 g

50. Rib-Eye Steak

Preparation Time: 5 min   **Cooking Time:** 14 min   **Servings:** 2

Ingredients:

- 2 lean ribeye steaks medium-sized
- Salt and freshly ground black pepper to taste
- Microgreen salad to serve

Directions:

1. Let the air fryer preheat at 400°F. Pat dry steaks with paper towels.
2. Use any spice blend or just salt and pepper on steaks.
3. Generously on both sides of the steak.
4. Put steaks in the air fryer basket. Cook according to the rareness you want. Or cook for 14 minutes and flip after halftime.
5. Take out from the air fryer and let it rest for about 5 minutes.
6. Serve with microgreen salad.

Nutrition: Calories: 470 Protein: 45 g Fat: 31 g Carbs: 23 g

51. Beef Curry

Preparation Time: 15 min   **Cooking Time:** 10 min   **Servings:** 2

Ingredients:

- 1 tbsp. extra-virgin olive oil
- 1 small onion, thinly sliced
- 2 tsp. minced fresh ginger
- 3 garlic cloves, minced
- 2 tsp. ground coriander
- 1 tsp. ground cumin
- 1 jalapeño or serrano pepper, split lengthwise but not all the way through
- ¼ tsp. ground turmeric
- ¼ tsp. salt
- 1 lb. (454 g.) grass-fed sirloin tip steak, top round steak, or top sirloin steak, cut into bite-size pieces
- 2 tbsp. chopped fresh cilantro
- ¼ cup water

Directions:

1. In an air fryer oven, heat the oil over medium-high.
2. Add the onion, and cook for 3 to 5 minutes until browned and softened. Add the ginger and garlic, stirring continuously until fragrant, about 30 seconds.
3. In a small bowl, mix the coriander, cumin, jalapeño, turmeric, and salt. Add the spice mixture to the skillet and stir continuously for 1 minute. Deglaze the skillet with about ¼ cup of water.
4. Add the beef and stir continuously for about 5 minutes until well-browned yet still medium-rare. Remove the jalapeño. Serve topped with cilantro.

Nutrition: Calories: 140 Fat: 7 g Protein: 18 g Carbs: 3 g Sugars: 1 g Fiber: 1 g Sodium: 141 mg

52. Sunday Pot Roast

Preparation Time: 10 min   **Cooking Time:** 1 h 45 min   **Servings:** 4

Ingredients:

- 1 (3 to 4 lb./1.4 to 1.8 kg.) beef rump roast
- 2 tsp. kosher salt, divided
- 2 tbsp. avocado oil
- 1 large onion, coarsely chopped (about 1½ cup)
- 4 large carrots, each cut into 4 pieces
- 1 tbsp. minced garlic
- 3 cups low-sodium beef broth
- 1 tsp. freshly ground black pepper
- 1 tbsp. dried parsley
- 2 tbsp. all-purpose flour

Directions:

1. Rub the roast all over with 1 tsp. salt.
2. Preheat the air fryer oven to 400°F (205°C).
3. Pour in the avocado oil. Carefully, place the roast in the pot and sear it for 6 to 9 minutes on each side. (You want a dark caramelized crust.) Hit "Cancel."
4. Transfer the roast from the pot to a plate.
5. In order, put the onion, carrots, and garlic in the pot. Place the roast on top of the vegetables along with any juices that accumulated on the plate.
6. In a medium bowl, whisk together the broth, remaining 1 tsp. of salt, pepper, and parsley. Pour the broth mixture over the roast.
7. Close and lock the lid of the air fryer. Set the valve to sealing.
8. Cook on high pressure for 1 hour and 30 minutes.
9. When the cooking is completed, hit "Cancel" and allow the pressure to release naturally.
10. Once the pin drops, unlock and remove the lid.
11. Using large slotted spoons, transfer the roast and vegetables to a serving platter while you make the gravy.
12. Using a large spoon or fat separator, remove the fat from the juices in the pot. Set the electric pressure cooker to the "Sauté" setting and bring the liquid to a boil.
13. In a small bowl, whisk together the flour and 4 tbsp. of water to make a slurry. Pour the slurry into the pot, whisking occasionally, until the gravy is the thickness you like. Season with salt and pepper, if necessary.
14. Serve the meat and carrots with the gravy.

Nutrition: Calories: 245 Fat: 10 g Protein: 33 g Carbs: 6 g Sugars: 2 g Fiber: 1 g Sodium: 397 mg

53. Beef and Pepper Fajita Bowls

Preparation Time: 10 min   **Cooking Time:** 15 min   **Servings:** 4

Ingredients:

- 4 tbsp. extra-virgin olive oil, divided
- 1 head cauliflower, riced
- 1 lb. (454 g) sirloin steak, cut into ¼-inch-thick strips
- 1 red bell pepper, seeded and sliced
- 1 onion, thinly sliced
- 2 garlic cloves, minced
- 2 limes juice
- 1 tsp. chili powder

Directions:

1. Preheat the air fryer oven to 400°F (205°C).
2. Heat 2 tbsp. of olive oil until it shimmers.
3. Add the cauliflower. Cook, stirring occasionally, until it softens, about 3 minutes. Set aside.
4. Add the remaining 2 tbsp. of oil to the air fryer, and heat it on medium-high until it shimmers.
5. Add the steak and cook, stirring occasionally, until it browns, about 3 minutes. Use a slotted spoon to remove the steak from the oil in the pan and set it aside.
6. Add the bell pepper and onion to the pan. Cook, stirring occasionally, until they start to brown, about 5 minutes.
7. Add the garlic and cook, stirring constantly, for 30 seconds.
8. Return the beef along with any juices that have been collected and the cauliflower to the pan. Add the lime juice and chili powder. Cook, stirring, until everything is warmed through, 2 to 3 minutes.

Nutrition: Calories: 310 Fat: 18 g Protein: 27 g Carbs: 13 g Sugars: 2 g Fiber: 3 g Sodium: 93 mg

54. Loaded Cottage Pie

Preparation Time: 15 min   **Cooking Time:** 1 hour   **Servings:** 6 to 8

Ingredients:

- large russet potatoes, peeled and halved
- 3 tbsp. extra-virgin olive oil, divided
- 1 small onion, chopped
- 1 bunch collard greens, stemmed and thinly sliced
- 2 carrots, peeled and chopped
- 2 medium tomatoes, chopped
- 1 garlic clove, minced

- 1 lb. (454 g.) 90 percent lean ground beef
- ½ cup chicken broth
- 1 tsp. Worcestershire sauce
- 1 tsp. celery seeds
- 1 tsp. smoked paprika
- ½ tsp. dried chives
- ½ tsp. ground mustard
- ½ tsp. cayenne pepper

Directions:

1. Preheat the oven to 400°F (205°C).
2. Bring a large pot of water to a boil.
3. Add the potatoes, and boil for 15 to 20 minutes, or until fork-tender.
4. Transfer the potatoes to a large bowl and mash with 1 tbsp. of olive oil.
5. In a large cast-iron skillet, heat the remaining 2 tbsp. of olive oil.
6. Add the onion, collard greens, carrots, tomatoes, and garlic and sauté, stirring often, for 7 to 10 minutes, or until the vegetables are softened.
7. Add the beef, broth, Worcestershire sauce, celery seeds, and smoked paprika.
8. Spread the meat and vegetable mixture evenly onto the bottom of a casserole dish. Sprinkle the chives, ground mustard, and cayenne on top of the mixture. Spread the mashed potatoes evenly over the top.
9. Transfer the casserole dish to the oven, and bake for 30 minutes, or until the top is light golden brown.

Nutrition: calories: 440 | fat: 17g | protein: 27g | carbs: 48g | sugars: 6g | fiber: 9g | sodium: 107mg

55. Low-fat Steak

Preparation Time: 25 min   **Cooking Time:** 10 min   **Servings:** 3

Ingredients:

- 400 g beef steak
- 1 tsp. white pepper
- 1 tsp. turmeric
- 1 tsp. cilantro
- 1 tsp. olive oil

- 3 tsp. lemon juice
- 1 tsp. oregano
- 1 tsp. salt
- 100 g water

Directions:

1. Rub the steaks with white pepper and turmeric and put them in the big bowl.
2. Sprinkle the meat with salt, oregano, cilantro, and lemon juice.
3. Leave the steak for 20 minutes.
4. Combine olive oil and water and pour it into the bowl with steaks.
5. Grill the steaks in the air fryer for 10 minutes from both sides.
6. Serve it immediately.

Nutrition: Caloric content–268 kcal Proteins–40.7 grams Fats–10.1 grams Carbohydrates–1.4 grams

56. Beef with Mushrooms

Preparation Time: 15 min   **Cooking Time:** 40 min   **Servings:** 4

Ingredients:

- 300 g beef
- 150 g mushrooms
- 1 onion
- 1 tsp. olive oil

- 100 g vegetable broth
- 1 tsp. basil
- 1 tsp. chili
- 30 g tomato juice

Directions:

1. For this recipe, you should take a solid piece of beef. Take the beef and pierce the meat with a knife.
2. Rub it with olive oil, basil, and chili, and lemon juice.
3. Chop the onion and mushrooms and pour them with vegetable broth.
4. Cook the vegetables for 5 minutes.
5. Take a big tray and put the meat in it. Add vegetable broth to the tray too. It will make the meat juicy.
6. Preheat the air fryer oven to 180°C and cook it for 35 minutes.

Nutrition: Caloric content – 175 kcal Proteins – 24.9 grams Fats – 6.2 grams Carbohydrates – 4.4 grams

CHAPTER 6:

Pork

---

57. Country-Style Pork Ribs

Preparation Time: 5 min   **Cooking Time:** 20–25 min   **Servings:** 4

Ingredients:

- 12 country-style pork ribs, trimmed excess fat
- 2 tbsp. cornstarch
- 2 tbsp. olive oil
- 1 tsp. dry mustard
- ½ tsp. thyme
- ½ tsp. garlic powder
- 1 tsp. dried marjoram
- Pinch salt
- Freshly ground black pepper, to taste

Directions:

1. Place the ribs on a clean work surface.
2. In a small bowl, combine the cornstarch, olive oil, mustard, thyme, garlic powder, marjoram, salt, and pepper, and rub into the ribs.
3. Place the ribs in the air fryer basket and roast at 400°F (204°C) for 10 minutes.
4. Carefully, turn the ribs using tongs and roast for 10 to 15 minutes or until the ribs are crisp and register an internal temperature of at least 150°F (66°C).

Nutrition: Calories: 579 Fat: 44 g Protein: 40 g Carbs: 4 g Fiber: 0 g Sugar: 0 g Sodium: 155 mg

58. Lemon and Honey Pork Tenderloin

Preparation Time: 5 min   **Cooking Time:** 10 min   **Servings:** 4

Ingredients:

- 1 (1 lb./454 g.) pork tenderloin, cut into ½-inch slices
- 1 tbsp. olive oil
- 1 tbsp. freshly squeezed lemon juice
- 1 tbsp. honey
- ½ tsp. grated lemon zest
- ½ tsp. dried marjoram
- Pinch salt
- Freshly ground black pepper to taste

Directions:

1. Put the pork tenderloin slices in a medium bowl.
2. In a small bowl, combine the olive oil, lemon juice, honey, lemon zest, marjoram, salt, and pepper. Mix.
3. Pour this marinade over the tenderloin slices and massage gently with your hands to work it into the pork.
4. Place the pork in the air fryer basket and roast at 400°F (204°C) for 10 minutes or until the pork registers at least 145°F (63°C) using a meat thermometer.

Nutrition: Calories: 208 Fat: 8 g Protein: 30 g Carbs: 5 g Fiber: 0 g Sugar: 4 g Sodium: 104 mg

59. Pork Burgers with Red Cabbage Slaw

Preparation Time: 20 min   **Cooking Time:** 7–9 min   **Servings:** 4

Ingredients:

- ½ cup Greek yogurt
- 2 tbsp. low-sodium mustard, divided
- 1 tbsp. freshly squeezed lemon juice
- ¼ cup sliced red cabbage
- ¼ cup grated carrots
- 1 lb. (454 g.) lean ground pork
- ½ tsp. paprika
- 1 cup mixed baby lettuce greens
- 2 small tomatoes, sliced
- 8 small low-sodium whole-wheat sandwich buns, cut in half

Directions:

1. In a small bowl, combine the yogurt, 1 tbsp. mustard, lemon juice, cabbage, and carrots; mix and refrigerate.
2. In a medium bowl, combine the pork, the remaining 1 tbsp. mustard, and paprika. Form into 8 small patties.
3. Put the patties into the air fryer basket. Air fry at 400°F (204°C) for 7 to 9 minutes, or until the patties register 165°F (74°C) as tested with a meat thermometer.
4. Assemble the burgers by placing some of the lettuce greens on a bun bottom. Top with a tomato slice, the patties, and the cabbage mixture. Add the bun top and serve immediately.

Nutrition: Calories: 473 Fat: 15 g Protein: 35 g Carbs: 51 g Fiber: 8 g Sugar: 8 g Sodium: 138 mg

60. Breaded Pork Chops

Preparation Time: 10 min **Cooking Time:** 12 min **Servings:** 4

Ingredients:

- 1 cup Whole-wheat breadcrumbs
- Salt ¼ tsp.
- 2–4 pcs. pork chops (center cut and boneless)
- ½ tsp. chili powder
- 1 tbsp. parmesan cheese
- 1½ tsp. paprika
- 1 egg beaten
- ½ tsp. onion powder
- ½ tsp. grounded garlic
- Pepper to taste

Directions:

1. Let the air fryer preheat to 400°F
2. Rub kosher salt on each side of pork chops, let it rest
3. Add beaten egg in a big bowl
4. Add Parmesan cheese, breadcrumbs, garlic, pepper, paprika, chili powder, and onion powder in a bowl and mix well
5. Dip pork chop in egg, then in breadcrumb mixture
6. Put it in the air fryer and spray it with oil.
7. Let it cook for 12 minutes at 400°F. Flip it over halfway through. Cook for another 6 minutes.
8. Serve with a side of salad.

Nutrition: Calories: 425 Fat: 20 g Fiber: 5 g Protein: 31 g Carbs: 19 g

61. Pork Taquitos in Air Fryer

Preparation Time: 10 min **Cooking Time:** 7-10 min **Servings:** 2

Ingredients:

- 3 cups pork tenderloin, cooked and shredded
- Cooking spray
- 2 ½ shredded mozzarella, fat-free
- 10 small tortillas
- 1 lime juice

Directions:

1. Let the air fryer preheat to 380°F.
2. Add lime juice to pork and mix well.
3. With a damp towel over the tortilla, microwave for 10 seconds to soften.
4. Add pork filling and cheese on top in a tortilla, roll up the tortilla tightly.
5. Place tortillas on a greased foil pan
6. Spray oil over tortillas. Cook for 7 to 10 minutes or until tortillas are golden brown, flip halfway through.
7. Serve with fresh salad.

Nutrition: Calories: 253 Fat: 18 g Carbs: 10 g Protein: 20 g

62. Pork Dumplings

Preparation Time: 30 min   **Cooking Time:** 20 min   **Servings:** 4

Ingredients:

- 18 dumpling wrappers
- 1 tsp. olive oil
- 4 cups bok choy (chopped)
- 2 tbsp. rice vinegar
- 1 tbsp. diced ginger
- ¼ tsp. crushed red pepper
- 1 tbsp. diced garlic
- ½ cup lean ground pork
- Cooking spray
- 2 tsp. lite soy sauce
- ½ tsp. honey
- 1 tsp. Toasted sesame oil
- ⅛ cup finely chopped scallions

Directions:

1. Preheat the air fryer oven to 400°F (205°C).
2. Add bok choy, cook for 6 minutes, and add garlic, ginger, and cook for 1 minute. Move this mixture on a paper towel, and pat dry the excess oil
3. In a bowl, add bok choy mixture, crushed red pepper, and lean ground pork and mix well.
4. Lay a dumpling wrapper on a plate and add 1 tbsp. of filling in the wrapper's middle. With water, seal the edges and crimp them.
5. Spray oil on the air fryer basket, add dumplings in it, and cook at 375°F for 12 minutes or until browned.
6. In the meantime, to make the sauce, add sesame oil, rice vinegar, scallions, soy sauce, and honey in a bowl mix together.
7. Serve the dumplings with sauce.

Nutrition: Calories: 140 Fat: 5 g Protein: 12 g Carbs: 9 g

63. Pork Chop & Broccoli

Preparation Time: 20 min   **Cooking Time:** 10 min   **Servings:** 2

Ingredients:

- 2 cups broccoli florets
- 2 pcs. bone-in pork chop
- ½ tsp. paprika
- 2 tbsp. avocado oil
- ½ tsp. garlic powder
- ½ tsp. onion powder
- 2 cloves crushed garlic
- 1 tsp. salt divided
- Cooking spray

Directions:

1. Let the air fryer preheat to 350°F. Spray the basket with cooking oil
2. Add 1 tbsp. avocado oil, onion powder, ½ tsp. of salt, garlic powder, and paprika in a bowl, mix well, rub this spice mix to the pork chop's sides
3. Add pork chops to air fryer basket and let it cook for 5 minutes
4. In the meantime, add 1 remaining tsp. of avocado oil, garlic, the other ½ tsp. of salt, and broccoli to a bowl and coat well
5. Flip the pork chop and add the broccoli. Let it cook for 5 more minutes.
6. Take out from the air fryer and serve.

Nutrition: Calories: 483 Fat: 20 g Carbs: 12 g Protein: 23 g

64. Cheesy Pork Chops

Preparation Time: 5 min   **Cooking Time:** 4 min   **Servings:** 2

Ingredients:

- 4 lean pork chops
- ½ tsp. salt
- ½ tsp. garlic powder
- 4 tbsp. shredded cheese
- 2 chopped cilantros

Directions:

1. Let the air fryer preheat to 350°F.
2. With garlic, cilantro, and salt, rub the pork chops. Put in the air fryer. Let it cook for 4 minutes.
3. Flip them and cook for 2 more minutes.
4. Add cheese on top of them and cook for another 2 minutes or until the cheese is melted.
5. Serve with salad greens.

Nutrition: Calories: 467 Protein: 61 g Fat: 22 g Saturated Fat: 8 g

65. Pork Rind Nachos

Preparation Time: 5 min   **Cooking Time:** 5 min   **Servings:** 2

Ingredients:

- 2 tbsp. pork rinds
- ¼ cup shredded cooked chicken
- ½ cup shredded Monterey jack cheese
- ¼ cup sliced pickled jalapeños
- ¼ cup guacamole
- ¼ cup full-fat sour cream

Directions:

1. Put pork rinds in a 6-inches round baking pan. Fill with grilled chicken and Monterey cheese jack. Place the pan in the basket with the air fryer.
2. Set the temperature to 370°F and set the timer for 5 minutes or until the cheese has been melted.
3. Eat right away with jalapeños, guacamole, and sour cream.

Nutrition: Calories: 295 Protein: 30.1 g Fiber: 1.2 g Carbs: 1.8 g Fat: 27.5 g Carbs: 3.0 g

66. Diet Boiled Ribs

Preparation Time: 10 min   **Cooking Time:** 30 min   **Servings:** 4

Ingredients:

- 400 g pork ribs
- 1 tsp. black pepper
- 1 g bay leaf
- 1 tsp. basil
- 1 white onion
- 1 carrot
- 1 tsp. cumin
- 700 ml of water

Directions:

1. Cut the ribs on the portions and sprinkle them with black pepper.
2. Take a big saucepan and pour water into it.
3. Add the ribs and bay leaf.
4. Peel the onion and carrot and add them to the water with meat.
5. Sprinkle it with cumin and basil.
6. Cook it on medium heat in the air fryer for 30 minutes.

Nutrition: Caloric content: 294 kcal, Proteins: 27.1 g Fats: 17.9 g Carbohydrates: 4.8 g

67. Quick & Juicy Pork Chops

Preparation Time: 10 min　　　**Cooking Time:** 12 min　　　**Servings:** 4

Ingredients:

- pork chops
- 1 tsp. olive oil
- 1 tsp. onion powder
- 1 tsp. paprika
- Pepper
- Salt

Directions:

1. Cover pork chops with olive oil and season with paprika, onion powder, pepper, and salt.
2. Place the dehydrating tray in a multi-level air fryer basket and place the basket in the instant pot.
3. Place pork chops on dehydrating tray.
4. Seal pot with air fryer lid and select air fry mode then set the temperature to 380°F and timer for 12 minutes. Turn pork chops halfway through.
5. Serve and enjoy.

Nutrition: Calories 270 Fat 21.1 g Carbohydrates 0.8 g Sugar 0.3 g Protein 18.1 g Cholesterol 69 mg

68. Perfect Pork Chops

Preparation Time: 10 min　　　**Cooking Time:** 15 min　　　**Servings:** 4

Ingredients:

- pork chops
- Pepper
- Salt

Directions:

1. Season pork chops with pepper and salt.
2. Place the dehydrating tray in a multi-level air fryer basket and place the basket in the instant pot.
3. Place pork chops on dehydrating tray.
4. Seal pot with air fryer lid and select air fry mode then set the temperature to 400°F and timer for 15 minutes. Turn pork chops halfway through.
5. Serve and enjoy.

Nutrition: Calories 256 Fat 19.9 g Carbohydrates 0 g Sugar 0 g Protein 18 g Cholesterol 69 mg

CHAPTER 7:

Lamb

69. Greek Lamb Pita Pockets

Preparation Time: 15 min   **Cooking Time:** 5–7 min   **Servings:** 4

Ingredients:
Dressing:
- 1 cup plain Greek yogurt
- 1 tbsp. lemon juice
- 1 tsp. dried dill weed, crushed
- 1 tsp. ground oregano
- ½ tsp. salt

Meatballs:
- ½ lb. (227 g.) ground lamb
- 1 tbsp. diced onion
- 1 tsp. dried parsley
- 1 tsp. dried dill weed, crushed
- ¼ tsp. oregano
- ¼ tsp. coriander
- ¼ tsp. ground cumin
- ¼ tsp. salt
- 4 pita halves

Suggested Toppings:
- Red onion, slivered
- Seedless cucumber, thinly sliced
- Crumbled feta cheese
- Sliced black olives
- Chopped fresh peppers

Directions:
1. Stir dressing ingredients together and refrigerate while preparing lamb.
2. Combine all meatball ingredients in a large bowl and stir to distribute seasonings.
3. Shape the meat mixture into 12 small meatballs, rounded or slightly flattened if you prefer.
4. Air fry at 390°F (199°C) for 5 to 7 minutes, until well done. Remove and drain on paper towels.
5. To serve, pile meatballs and your choice of toppings in pita pockets and drizzle with dressing.

Nutrition: Calories: 270 Fat: 14 g Protein: 18 g Carbs: 18 g Fiber: 2 g Sugar: 2 g Sodium: 618 mg

70. Rosemary Lamb Chops

Preparation Time: 30 min   **Cooking Time:** 20 min   **Servings:** 2-3

Ingredients:

- 2 tsp. oil
- ½ tsp. ground rosemary
- ½ tsp. lemon juice

- 1 lb. (454 g.) lamb chops, approximately 1-inch thick
- Salt and pepper to taste
- Cooking spray

Directions:

1. Mix the oil, rosemary, and lemon juice and rub them into all sides of the lamb chops. Season to taste with salt and pepper.
2. For best flavor, cover lamb chops and allow them to rest in the fridge for 15 to 20 minutes.
3. Spray air fryer basket with non-stick spray and place lamb chops in it.
4. Air fry at 360°F (182°C) for approximately 20 minutes. This will cook chops to medium. The meat will be juicy but have no remaining pink. Air fry for 1 to 2 minutes longer for well-done chops. For rare chops, continue cooking for about 12 minutes and check for doneness.

Nutrition: Calories: 237 Fat: 13 g Protein: 30 g Carbs: 0 g Fiber: 0 g Sugar 0 g Sodium: 116 mg

71. Herb Butter Lamb Chops

Preparation Time: 10 min   **Cooking Time:** 5 min   **Servings:** 4

Ingredients:

- 4 lamb chops
- 1 tsp. rosemary, diced
- 1 tbsp. butter

- Pepper
- Salt

Directions:

1. Season lamb chops with pepper and salt.
2. Place the dehydrating tray in a multi-level air fryer basket and insert the basket in the air fryer oven.
3. Place lamb chops on dehydrating tray.
4. Seal pot with air fryer lid and select "Air Fry" mode, then set the temperature to 400°F and timer for 5 minutes.
5. Mix butter and rosemary and spread overcooked lamb chops.
6. Serve and enjoy.

Nutrition: Calories: 278 Fat: 12.8 g Carbs: 0.2 g Sugar: 0 g Protein: 38 g Cholesterol: 129 mg

72. Za'atar Lamb Chops

Preparation Time: 10 min　　　**Cooking Time:** 10 min　　　**Servings:** 4

Ingredients:

- 4 lamb loin chops
- ½ tbsp. Za'atar
- 1 tbsp. fresh lemon juice
- 1 tsp. olive oil
- 2 garlic cloves, minced
- Pepper
- Salt

Directions:

1. Coat lamb chops with oil and lemon juice and rub with Za'atar, garlic, pepper, and salt.
2. Place the dehydrating tray in a multi-level air fryer basket and insert the basket in the air fryer oven.
3. Place lamb chops on dehydrating tray.
4. Seal pot with air fryer lid and select air fry mode, then set the temperature to 400°F and timer for 10 minutes. Turn lamb chops halfway through.
5. Serve and enjoy.

Nutrition: Calories: 266 Fat: 11.2 g Carbs: 0.6 g Sugar: 0.1 g Protein: 38 g Cholesterol: 122 mg

73. Greek Lamb Chops

Preparation Time: 10 min　　　**Cooking Time:** 10 min　　　**Servings:** 4

Ingredients:

- 2 lb. lamb chops
- 2 tsp. garlic, minced
- 1 ½ tsp. dried oregano
- ¼ cup fresh lemon juice
- ¼ cup olive oil
- ½ tsp. pepper
- 1 tsp. salt

Directions:

1. Add lamb chops in a mixing bowl. Add remaining ingredients over the lamb chops and coat well.
2. Arrange lamb chops on the air fryer oven tray and cook at 400°F for 5 minutes.
3. Turn lamb chops and cook for 5 more minutes.
4. Serve and enjoy.

Nutrition: Calories: 538 Fat: 29.4 g Carbs: 1.3 g Protein: 64 g

74. Herbed Lamb Chops

Preparation Time: 1h   **Cooking Time:** 13 min   **Servings:** 4

Ingredients:
- 1 lb. lamb chops, pastured

For the Marinate:
- 2 tbsp. lemon juice
- 1 tsp. dried rosemary
- 1 tsp. salt
- 1 tsp. dried thyme
- 1 tsp. coriander
- 1 tsp. dried oregano
- 2 tbsp. olive oil

Directions:
1. Prepare the marinade and for this, place all its ingredients in a bowl and whisk until combined.
2. Pour the marinade into a large plastic bag, add lamb chops in it, seal the bag, then turn it upside down to coat lamb chops with the marinade and let it in the refrigerator for a minimum of 1 hour.
3. Then switch on the air fryer, insert the fryer basket, grease it with olive oil, then shut with its lid, set the fryer at 390°F, and preheat for 5 minutes.
4. Open the fryer, add marinated lamb chops in it, close with its lid and cook for 8 minutes until nicely golden and cooked, turning the lamb chops halfway through the frying.
5. When the air fryer beeps, open its lid, transfer lamb chops to a plate and serve.

Nutrition: Calories: 177.4 Carbs: 1.7 g Fat: 8 g Protein: 23.4 g Fiber: 0.5 g

75. Spicy Lamb Sirloin Steak

Preparation Time: 40 min   **Cooking Time:** 20 min   **Servings:** 4

Ingredients:

- 1 lb. lamb sirloin steaks, pastured, boneless

For the Marinade:

- ½ white onion, peeled
- 1 tsp. ground fennel
- 5 garlic cloves, peeled
- 4 slices ginger
- 1 tsp. salt

- ½ tsp. ground cardamom
- 1 tsp. garam masala
- 1 tsp. ground cinnamon
- 1 tsp. cayenne pepper

Directions:

1. Place all the ingredients for the marinade in a food processor and then pulse until well blended.
2. Make cuts in the lamb chops by using a knife, then place them in a large bowl and add prepared marinade in it.
3. Mix well until lamb chops are coated with the marinade and let them in the refrigerator for a minimum of 30 minutes.
4. Then switch on the air fryer, insert the fryer basket, grease it with olive oil, then shut with its lid, set the fryer at 330°F, and preheat for 5 minutes.
5. Open the fryer, add lamb chops in it, close with its lid and cook for 15 minutes until nicely golden and cooked, flipping the steaks halfway through the frying.
6. When the air fryer beeps, open its lid, transfer lamb steaks to a plate and serve.

Nutrition: Calories: 182 Carbs: 3 g Fat: 7 g Protein: 24 g Fiber: 1 g

76. Garlic Rosemary Lamb Chops

Preparation Time: 1 hour   **Cooking Time:** 12 min   **Servings:** 4

Ingredients:

- 4 lamb chops, pastured
- 1 tsp. ground black pepper
- 2 tsp. minced garlic
- 1 ½ tsp. salt
- 2 tsp. olive oil
- 4 garlic cloves, peeled
- 4 rosemary sprigs

Directions:

1. Take the fryer pan, place lamb chops in it, season the top with ½ tsp. black pepper and ¾ tsp. salt, then drizzle evenly with oil and spread with 1 tsp. minced garlic.
2. Add garlic cloves and rosemary and then let the lamb chops marinate in the pan into the refrigerator for a minimum of 1 hour.
3. Then switch on the air fryer, insert the fryer pan, then shut with its lid, set the fryer at 360°F, and cook for 6 minutes.
4. Flip the lamb chops, season them with remaining salt and black pepper, add remaining minced garlic, and continue cooking for 6 minutes or until lamb chops are cooked.
5. When the air fryer beeps, open its lid, transfer lamb chops to a plate and serve.

Nutrition: Calories: 616 Carbs: 1 g Fat: 28 g Protein: 83 g Fiber: 0.3 g

---

77. Cherry-Glazed Lamb Chops

Preparation Time: 10 min   **Cooking Time:** 20 min   **Servings:** 4

Ingredients:

- 4 (4 oz./113 g) lamb chops
- 1½ tsp. chopped fresh rosemary
- ¼ tsp. salt
- ¼ tsp. freshly ground black pepper
- 1 cup frozen cherries, thawed
- ¼ cup dry red wine
- 2 tbsp. orange juice
- 1 tsp. extra-virgin olive oil

Directions:

1. Season the lamb chops with rosemary, salt, and pepper.
2. In a small saucepan over medium-low heat, combine the cherries, red wine, and orange juice, and simmer, stirring regularly, until the sauce thickens, 8 to 10 minutes.
3. Heat a large skillet over medium-high heat. When the pan is hot, add the olive oil to lightly coat the bottom.
4. Cook the lamb chops for 3 to 4 minutes on each side until well-browned yet medium-rare.
5. Serve topped with the cherry glaze.

Nutrition: Calories: 356 Fat: 27 g Protein: 20 g Carbs: 6 g Sugars: 4 g Fiber: 1 g Sodium: 199 mg

78. Lamb and Vegetable Stew

Preparation Time: 10 min   **Cooking Time:** 3–6 hours   **Servings:** 3

Ingredients:

- 1 lb. (454 g.) boneless lamb stew meat
- 1 lb. (454 g.) turnips, peeled, and chopped
- 1 fennel bulb, trimmed and thinly sliced
- 10 oz. (283 g.) mushrooms, sliced
- 1 onion, diced
- 3 garlic cloves, minced
- 2 cups low-sodium chicken broth
- 2 tbsp. tomato paste
- ¼ cup dry red wine (optional)
- 1 tsp. chopped fresh thyme
- ½ tsp. salt
- ¼ tsp. freshly ground black pepper
- Chopped fresh parsley to garnish

Directions:

1. In a slow cooker, combine the lamb, turnips, fennel, mushrooms, onion, garlic, chicken broth, tomato paste, red wine (if using), thyme, salt, and pepper.
2. Cover and cook on high for 3 hours or on low for 6 hours. When the meat is tender and falling apart, garnish with parsley and serve.
3. If you don't have a slow cooker, in a large pot, heat 2 tsp. of olive oil over medium heat, and sear the lamb on all sides. Remove from the pot and set aside.
4. Add the turnips, fennel, mushrooms, onion, and garlic to the pot, and cook for 3 to 4 minutes until the vegetables begin to soften.
5. Add the chicken broth, tomato paste, red wine (if using), thyme, salt, pepper, and browned lamb. Bring to a boil, then reduce the heat to low. Simmer for 1½ to 2 hours until the meat is tender. Garnish with parsley and serve.

Nutrition: Calories: 303 Fat: 7 g Protein: 32 g Carbs: 27 g Sugars: 7 g Fiber: 4 g Sodium: 310 mg

79. Lime-Parsley Lamb Cutlets

Preparation Time: 10 min   **Cooking Time:** 10 min   **Servings:** 4

Ingredients:

- ¼ cup extra-virgin olive oil
- ¼ cup freshly squeezed lime juice
- 2 tbsp. lime zest
- 2 tbsp. chopped fresh parsley
- Pinch sea salt
- Pinch freshly ground black pepper
- 12 lamb cutlets (about 1½ lb./680 g total)

Directions:

1. In a medium bowl, whisk together the oil, lime juice, zest, parsley, salt, and pepper.
2. Transfer the marinade to a resealable plastic bag.
3. Add the cutlets to the bag and remove as much air as possible before sealing.
4. Marinate the lamb in the refrigerator for about 4 hours, turning the bag several times.
5. Preheat the oven to broil.
6. Remove the chops from the bag and arrange them on an aluminum foil-lined baking sheet. Discard the marinade.
7. Broil the chops for 4 minutes per side for medium doneness.
8. Let the chops rest for 5 minutes before serving.

Nutrition: Calories: 413 Fat: 29 g Protein: 31 g Carbs: 1 g Sugars: 0 g Fiber: 0 g Sodium: 100 mg

CHAPTER 8:
Fish & Seafood

80. Salmon Cakes in Air Fryer

Preparation Time: 9 min   **Cooking Time:** 7 min   **Servings:** 2

Ingredients:
- 8 oz. fresh salmon fillet
- 1 egg
- ⅛ salt
- ¼ garlic powder
- 1 Sliced lemon

Directions:
1. In the bowl, chop the salmon, add the egg and spices.
2. Form tiny cakes.
3. Let the air fryer preheat to 390°F. On the bottom of the air fryer bowl lay sliced lemons—place cakes on top.
4. Cook them for 7 minutes. Based on your diet preferences, eat with your chosen dip.

Nutrition: Calories: 194 Fat: 9 g Carbs: 1 g Proteins: 25 g

81. Crispy Fish Sticks in Air Fryer

Preparation Time: 9 min   **Cooking Time:** 10 min   **Servings:** 4

Ingredients:
- 1 lb. whitefish such as cod
- ¼ cup mayonnaise
- 2 tbsp. Dijon mustard
- 2 tbsp. water
- 1 ½ cup pork rind
- ¾ tsp. Cajun seasoning
- Kosher salt and pepper to taste
- Cooking spray

Directions:
1. Spray with non-stick cooking spray to the air fryer rack.
2. Pat the fish dry and cut into sticks about 1 inch by 2 inches' broad
3. Stir together the mayonnaise, mustard, and water in a tiny small dish. Mix the pork rinds and Cajun seasoning into another small container.
4. Adding kosher salt and pepper to taste (both pork rinds and seasoning can have a decent amount of kosher salt, so you can dip a finger to see how salty it is).
5. Working for one slice of fish at a time, dip to cover in the mayonnaise mix, and then tap off the excess. Dip into the mixture of pork rind, then flip to cover. Place on the rack of an air fryer.
6. Set at 400°F to air fry for 5 minutes, then turn the fish with tongs and bake for another 5 minutes. Serve.

Nutrition: Calories: 263 Fat: 16 g Carbs: 1 g Proteins: 26.4 g

82. Basil-Parmesan Crusted Salmon

Preparation Time: 5 min   **Cooking Time:** 7 min   **Servings:** 4

Ingredients:

- 3 tbsp. grated Parmesan
- 4 skinless salmon fillets
- ¼ tsp. salt
- Freshly ground black pepper

- 3 tbsp. low-fat mayonnaise
- ¼ cup basil leaves, chopped
- ½ lemon

Directions:

1. Let the air fryer preheat to 400°F. Spray the basket with olive oil.
2. With salt, pepper, and lemon juice, season the salmon.
3. In a bowl, mix 2 tbsp. of Parmesan cheese with mayonnaise and basil leaves.

4. Add this mix and more parmesan on top of salmon and cook for 7 minutes or until fully cooked.
5. Serve hot.

Nutrition: Calories: 289 Fat: 18.5 g Carbs: 1.5 g Proteins: 30 g

83. Cajun Shrimp in Air Fryer

Preparation Time: 9 min   **Cooking Time:** 3 min   **Servings:** 4

Ingredients:

- 24 extra-jumbo shrimp, peeled,
- 2 tbsp. olive oil
- 1 tbsp. Cajun seasoning
- 1 zucchini, thick slices (half-moons)

- ¼ cup cooked turkey
- 2 yellow squash, sliced half-moons
- ¼ tsp. kosher salt

Directions:

1. In a bowl, mix the shrimp with Cajun seasoning.
2. In another bowl, add zucchini, turkey, salt, squash, and coat with oil.
3. Let the air fryer preheat to 400°F.

4. Move the shrimp and vegetable mix to the fryer basket and cook for 3 minutes.
5. Serve hot.

Nutrition: Calories: 284 Fat: 14 g Carbs: 8 g Proteins: 31 g

84. Crispy Air Fryer Fish

Preparation Time: 11 min   **Cooking Time:** 18 min   **Servings:** 4

Ingredients:

- 2 tsp. old bay
- 4–6, cut in half, whiting fish fillets
- ¼ cup fine cornmeal
- ¼ cup flour
- 1 tsp paprika
- ½ tsp. garlic powder
- 1 ½ tsp. salt
- ½ freshly ground black pepper

Directions:

1. In a Ziploc bag, add all ingredients and coat the fish fillets with it.
2. Spray oil on the basket of the air fryer and put the fish in it.
3. Cook for ten minutes at 400°F. Flip fish if necessary and coat with oil spray and cook for another 7 minutes.
4. Serve with salad green.

Nutrition: Calories: 254 Fat: 12.7 g Carbs: 8.2 g Proteins: 17.5 g

85. Air Fryer Lemon Cod

Preparation Time: 5 min   **Cooking Time:** 10 min   **Servings:** 1

Ingredients:

- 1 cod fillet
- 1 tbsp. chopped dried parsley
- Kosher salt and pepper to taste
- 1 tbsp. garlic powder
- 1 lemon

Directions:

1. In a bowl, mix all ingredients and coat the fish fillet with spices.
2. Slice the lemon and lay it at the bottom of the air fryer basket.
3. Put spiced fish on top. Cover the fish with lemon slices.
4. Cook for 10 minutes at 375°F, the internal temperature of the fish should be 145°F.
5. Serve.

Nutrition: Calories: 101 Fat: 1 g Carbs: 10 g Proteins: 16g

86. Air Fryer Salmon Fillets

Preparation Time: 5 min **Cooking Time:** 15 min **Servings:** 2

Ingredients:

- ¼ cup low-fat Greek yogurt
- 2 salmon fillets
- 1 tbsp. fresh dill (chopped)
- 1 lemon juice
- ½ garlic powder
- Kosher salt and pepper

Directions:

1. Cut the lemon into slices and lay it at the bottom of the air fryer basket.
2. Season the salmon with kosher salt and pepper. Put salmon on top of lemons.
3. Let it cook at 330°F for 15 minutes.
4. In the meantime, mix garlic powder, lemon juice, salt, pepper with yogurt and dill.
5. Serve the fish with sauce.

Nutrition: Calories: 194 Fat: 7 g Carbs: 6 g Proteins: 25 g

87. Air Fryer Fish and Chips

Preparation Time: 11 min **Cooking Time:** 35 min **Servings:** 4

Ingredients:

- 4 cups any fish fillet
- ¼ cup flour
- 1 cup whole-wheat breadcrumbs
- 1 egg
- 2 tbsp. oil
- 2 potatoes
- 1 tsp. salt

Directions:

1. Cut the potatoes in fries. Then coat with oil and salt.
2. Cook in the air fryer for 20 minutes at 400°F, toss the fries halfway through.
3. In the meantime, coat fish in flour, then in the whisked egg, and finally in breadcrumbs mix.
4. Place the fish in the air fryer and let it cook at 330°F for 15 minutes.
5. Flip it halfway through, if needed.
6. Serve with tartar sauce and salad green.

Nutrition: Calories: 409 Fat: 11 g Carbs: 44 g Proteins: 30 g

88. Air-Fried Fish Nuggets

Preparation Time: 15 min   **Cooking Time:** 12 min   **Servings:** 4

Ingredients:

- 2 cups (skinless) fish fillets in cubes
- 1 egg beaten
- 5 tbsp. flour
- 5 tbsp. water
- Kosher salt and pepper to taste
- ½ cup breadcrumbs mix
- ¼ cup whole-wheat breadcrumbs
- Oil for spraying

Directions:

1. Season the fish cubes with kosher salt and pepper.
2. In a bowl, add flour and gradually add water, mixing as you add.
3. Then mix in the egg. And keep mixing but do not over mix.
4. Coat the cubes in batter, then in the breadcrumb mix. Coat well.
5. Place the cubes in a baking tray and spray with oil.
6. Let the air fryer preheat to 200°C.
7. Place cubes in the air fryer and cook for 12 minutes or until well cooked and golden brown.
8. Serve with salad greens.

Nutrition: Calories: 184 Fat: 3 g Carbs: 10 g Proteins: 19 g

89. Garlic Rosemary Grilled Prawns

Preparation Time: 5 min   **Cooking Time:** 11 min   **Servings:** 2

Ingredients:

- ½ tbsp. melted butter
- 8 green capsicum slices
- 8 prawns
- ⅛ cup rosemary leaves
- Kosher salt and freshly ground black pepper
- 3-4 cloves minced garlic

Directions:

1. In a bowl, mix all the ingredients and marinate the prawns in it for at least 60 minutes or more.
2. Add 2 prawns and 2 slices of capsicum on each skewer.
3. Let the air fryer preheat to 180°C.
4. Cook for 5 to 6 minutes. Then change the temperature to 200°C and cook for another 5 minutes.
5. Serve with lemon wedges.

Nutrition: Calories: 194 Fat: 10 g Carbs: 12 g Proteins: 26 g

90. Asian-Inspired Swordfish Steaks

Preparation Time: 10 min   **Cooking Time:** 6 to 11 min   **Servings:** 4

Ingredients:

- 4- oz. / 113-g swordfish steaks
- ½ tsp. toasted sesame oil
- 1 jalapeño pepper, finely minced
- 2 garlic cloves, grated
- 1 tbsp. grated fresh ginger
- ½ tsp. Chinese five-spice powder
- ⅛ Teaspoon freshly ground black pepper
- 2 tbsp. freshly squeezed lemon juice

Directions:

1 Place the swordfish steaks on a work surface and drizzle with the sesame oil.
2 In a small bowl, mix the jalapeño, garlic, ginger, five-spice powder, pepper, and lemon juice. Rub this mixture into the fish and let it stand for 10 minutes. Put in the air fryer basket.
3 Roast at 380°F (193°C) for 6 to 11 minutes, or until the swordfish reaches an inner temperature of at least 140°F (60°C) on a meat thermometer. Serve immediately.

Nutrition: Calories: 188 Fat: 6g Protein: 29g Carbs: 2g Fiber: 0g Sugar 1g Sodium: 132mg

91. Salmon with Fennel and Carrot

Preparation Time: 15 min   **Cooking Time:** 13 min   **Servings:** 2

Ingredients:

- 1 fennel bulb, thinly sliced
- 1 large carrot, peeled and sliced
- 1 small onion, thinly sliced
- ¼ cup low-fat sour cream
- ¼ tsp. coarsely ground pepper
- 2 (5- oz. / 142-g) salmon fillets

Directions:

1 Combine the fennel, carrot, and onion in a bowl and toss.
2 Put the vegetable mixture into a baking pan. Prepare in the air fryer at 400°F (204°C) for 4 minutes or until the vegetables are crisp-tender.
3 Remove the pan from the air fryer. Stir in the sour cream and sprinkle the vegetables with the pepper.
4 Top with the salmon fillets.
5 Return the pan to the air fryer. Roast for another 9 to 10 minutes or until the salmon just barely flakes when tested with a fork.

Nutrition: Calories: 254 Fat: 9g Protein: 31g Carbs: 12g Fiber: 3g Sugar 5g Sodium: 115mg

92. Ginger and Green Onion Fish

Preparation Time: 15 min   **Cooking Time:** 15 min   **Servings:** 2

Ingredients:

Bean Sauce:

- 2 tbsp. low-sodium soy sauce
- 1 tbsp. rice wine
- 1 tbsp. doubanjiang (Chinese black bean paste)
- 1 tsp. minced fresh ginger
- 1 clove garlic, minced

Vegetables and Fish:

- 1 tbsp. peanut oil
- ¼ cup julienned green onions
- ¼ cup chopped fresh cilantro
- 2 tbsp. julienned fresh ginger
- 2 (6- oz. / 170-g.) white fish fillets, such as tilapia

Directions:

1   **For the sauce:** In a small bowl, combine all the ingredients and stir until well combined; set aside.

2   **For the vegetables and fish:** In a medium bowl, combine the peanut oil, green onions, cilantro, and ginger. Toss to combine.

3   Cut two squares of parchment large enough to hold one fillet and half of the vegetables. Place one fillet on each parchment square, top with the vegetables, and pour over the sauce. Bend over the parchment paper and tuck the sides in small, tight folds to hold the fish, vegetables, and sauce securely inside the packet.

4   Abode the packets in a single layer in the air fryer basket—roast at 350°F (177°C) for 15 minutes.

5   Transfer each packet to a dinner plate. Cut open with scissors just before serving.

Nutrition: Calories: 237 Fat: 9g Protein: 36g Carbs: 3g Fiber: 0g Sugar: 0g Sodium: 641mg

CHAPTER 9:
Vegetables

93. Fried Peppers with Sriracha Mayo

Preparation Time: 20 min **Cooking Time:** 10 min **Servings:** 2

Ingredients:

- bell peppers, seeded and sliced (1-inch pieces
- 1 onion, sliced (1-inch pieces
- 1 tbsp. olive oil
- ½ tsp. dried rosemary
- ½ tsp. dried basil
- Kosher salt, to taste
- ¼ tsp. ground black pepper
- ⅓ cup mayonnaise
- ⅓ tsp. Sriracha

Directions:

1 Fling the bell peppers and onions with olive oil, rosemary, basil, salt, and black pepper.
2 Place the peppers and onions on an even layer in the cooking basket. Cook at 400°F for 12 to 14 minutes.
3 Meanwhile, make the sauce by whisking the mayonnaise and Sriracha. Serve immediately.

Nutrition: 346 Calories 34.1g Fat 9.5g Carbs 2.3g Protein 4.9g Sugars

94. Corn on the Cob with Herb Butter

Preparation Time: 15 min **Cooking Time:** 10 min **Servings:** 2

Ingredients:

- 2 ears new corn, shucked and cut into halves
- 2 tbsp. butter, room temperature
- 1 tsp. granulated garlic
- ½ tsp. fresh ginger, grated
- Sea salt and pepper, to taste
- 1 tbsp. fresh rosemary, chopped
- 1 tbsp. fresh basil, chopped
- 2 tbsp. fresh chives, roughly chopped

Directions:

1 Spritz the corn with cooking spray. Cook at 395°F for 6 minutes, turning them over halfway through the cooking time.
2 For the time being, mix the butter with the granulated garlic, ginger, salt, black pepper, rosemary, and basil.
3 Spread the butter mixture all over the corn on the cob. Cook in the preheated Air Fryer for an additional 2 minutes. Bon appétit!

Nutrition: 239 Calories 13.3g Fat 30.2g Carbs 5.4g Protein 5.8g Sugars

95. American-Style Brussels Sprout Salad

Preparation Time: 35 min   **Cooking Time:** 10 min   **Servings:** 4

Ingredients:

- 1 lb. Brussels sprouts
- 1 apple, cored and diced
- ½ cup mozzarella cheese, crumbled
- ½ cup pomegranate seeds
- 1 small-sized red onion, chopped
- eggs, hardboiled and sliced

Dressing:

- ¼ cup olive oil
- 2 tbsp. champagne vinegar
- 1 tsp. Dijon mustard
- 1 tsp. honey
- Sea salt and ground black pepper, to taste

Directions:

1. Start by preheating your Air Fryer to 380°F.
2. Add the Brussels sprouts to the cooking basket. Spritz with cooking spray and cook for 15 minutes. Let it cool to room temperature for about 15 minutes.
3. Toss the Brussels sprouts with apple, cheese, pomegranate seeds, and red onion.
4. Mix all ingredients for the dressing and toss to combine well. Serve topped with hard-boiled eggs. Bon appétit!

Nutrition: 319 Calories 18.5g Fat 27g Carbs 14.7g Protein 14.6g Sugars

96. Three-Cheese Stuffed Mushrooms

Preparation Time: 15 min   **Cooking Time:** 10 min   **Servings:** 3

Ingredients:

- 2 large button mushrooms, stems removed
- 1 tbsp. olive oil
- Salt and ground black pepper, to taste
- ½ tsp. dried rosemary
- 1 tbsp. Swiss cheese shredded
- 2 tbsp. Romano cheese, shredded
- 1 tbsp. cream cheese
- 1 tsp. soy sauce
- 1 tsp. garlic, minced
- 1 tbsp. green onion, minced

Directions:

1. Brush the mushroom caps with olive oil; sprinkle with salt, pepper, and rosemary.
2. In a mixing bowl, thoroughly combine the remaining ingredients, combine them well, and divide the filling mixture among the mushroom caps.
3. Cook in the preheated Air Fryer at 390°F for 7 minutes.
4. Let the mushrooms cool slightly before serving. Bon appétit!

Nutrition: 345 Calories 28g Fat 11.2g Carbs 14.4g Protein 8.1g Sugars

97. Sweet Corn Fritters with Avocado

Preparation Time: 20 min

Cooking Time: 10 min   **Servings:** 3

Ingredients:

- 2 cups sweet corn kernels
- 1 small-sized onion, chopped
- 1 garlic clove, minced
- 2 eggs, whisked
- 1 tsp. baking powder
- 2 tbsp. fresh cilantro, chopped
- Sea salt and ground black pepper, to taste
- 1 avocado, peeled, pitted, and diced
- 2 tbsp. sweet chili sauce

Directions:

1. In a mixing bowl, thoroughly combine the corn, onion, garlic, eggs, baking powder, cilantro, salt, and black pepper.
2. Shape the corn mixture into 6 patties and transfer them to the lightly greased Air Fryer basket.
3. Cook in the preheated Air Fry at 370°for for 8 minutes; turn them over and cook for 7 minutes longer.
4. Serve the cakes with avocado and chili sauce.

Nutrition: 383 Calories 21.3g Fat 42.8g Carbs 12.7g Protein 9.2g Sugars

98. Greek-Style Vegetable Bake

Preparation Time: 35 min   **Cooking Time:** 10 min   **Servings:** 4

Ingredients:

- 1 eggplant, peeled and sliced
- 2 bell peppers, seeded and sliced
- 1 red onion, sliced
- 1 tsp. fresh garlic, minced
- 2 tbsp. olive oil
- 1 tsp. mustard
- 1 tsp. dried oregano
- 1 tsp. smoked paprika
- Salt and ground black pepper, to taste
- 1 tomato, sliced
- 4 oz. halloumi cheese, sliced lengthways

Directions:

1. Start by preheating your Air Fryer to 370°F. Spritz a baking pan with nonstick cooking spray.
2. Place the eggplant, peppers, onion, and garlic on the baking pan's bottom. Add the olive oil, mustard, and spices. Transfer to the cooking basket and cook for 14 minutes.
3. Top with the tomatoes and cheese; increase the temperature to 390°F and cook for 5 minutes more until bubbling. Let it sit on a cooling rack for 10 minutes before serving.
4. Bon appétit!

Nutrition: 296 Calories 22.9g Fat 16.1g Carbs 9.3g Protein 9.9g Sugars

99. Garlic-Roasted Bell Peppers

Preparation Time: 5 min   **Cooking Time:** 20 min   **Servings:** 4

Ingredients:

- 2 bell peppers, any colors, stemmed, seeded, membranes removed, and cut into fourths
- 1 tsp. olive oil
- 2 garlic cloves, minced
- ½ tsp. dried thyme

Directions:

1. Put the peppers in the basket of the air fryer and drizzle with olive oil. Toss gently. Roast for 15 minutes.
2. Sprinkle with garlic and thyme. Roast for 3 to 5 minutes more, or until tender. Serve immediately..

Nutrition: Calories: 36 Fat: 1g Protein: 1g Carbs: 5g Fiber: 2g

100. Sweet Beets Salad

Preparation Time: 20 min   **Cooking Time:** 15 min   **Servings:** 4

Ingredients:

- 1 ½-lb. beets; peeled and quartered
- 2 tbsps. brown sugar
- 2 scallions; chopped
- 2 tbsp. cider vinegar
- ½ cup orange juice
- 2 cups Arugula
- 2 tbsps. mustard
- A drizzle olive oil
- 2 tbsps. orange zest; grated

Directions:

1. Season the beets with orange juice and oil in a bowl.
2. Spread the beets in the air fryer basket and seal the fryer.
3. Cook the beet for 10 minutes at 350°F on Air fryer mode.
4. Place these cooked beets in a bowl then toss in orange zest, arugula, and scallions.
5. Whisk mustard, vinegar, and sugar in a different bowl.
6. Add this mixture to the beets and mix well.

Nutrition: Calories: 151 Fat: 2g Fiber: 4g, Carbs: 14g Protein: 4g

101. Veg Buffalo Cauliflower

Preparation Time: 20 min   **Cooking Time:** 15 min   **Servings:** 3

Ingredients:

- 1 medium head cauliflower
- 1 tsp. avocado oil
- 2 tbsp. red hot sauce
- 1 tbsp. nutritional yeast
- 1 ½ tsp. maple syrup
- ¼ tsp. sea salt
- 1 tbsp. cornstarch or arrowroot starch

Directions:

1. Set your air fryer toaster oven to 360°F. Place all the ingredients into a bowl except cauliflower. Mix them to combine.
2. Put the cauliflower and mix to coat equally. Put half of your cauliflower into an air fryer and cook for 15 minutes but keep shaking them until your get desired consistency.
3. Do the same for the cauliflower which is left except lower cooking time to 10 minutes.
4. Keep the cauliflower tightly sealed in the refrigerator for 3-4 days. For heating again add back to the air fryer for 1-2 minutes until crispness.

Nutrition: Calories: 248 Fat: 20g Protein: 4g Carbs: 13g Fiber: 2g

102. Eggplant Surprise

Preparation Time: 17 min   **Cooking Time:** 7 min   **Servings:** 4

Ingredients:

- 1 eggplant, roughly chopped
- 3 zucchinis, roughly chopped
- 3 tbsp. extra-virgin olive oil
- 3 tomatoes, sliced
- 2 tbsp. lemon juice
- 1 tsp. thyme, dried
- 1 tsp. oregano, dried
- Salt and black pepper to taste

Directions:

1. Put eggplant pieces in your air fryer oven.
2. Add zucchinis and tomatoes.
3. In a bowl, mix lemon juice with salt, pepper, thyme, oregano, and oil and stir well.
4. Pour this over veggie, toss to coat, seal the air fryer oven lid and cook at high for 7 minutes.
5. Quickly release the pressure, open the lid; divide among plates and serve.

Nutrition: Calories: 160 Fat: 7 g Protein: 1 g Sugar: 6 g Carbs: 19 g Fiber: 8 g Sodium: 20 mg

103. Carrots and Turnips

Preparation Time: 18 min   **Cooking Time:** 9 min   **Servings:** 4

Ingredients:

- 2 turnips, peeled and sliced
- 1 small onion; chopped.
- 1 tsp. lemon juice
- 1 tsp. cumin, ground.
- 3 carrots, sliced
- 1 tbsp. extra-virgin olive oil
- 1 cup water
- Salt and black pepper to the taste

Directions:

1. Set your air fryer oven on "Sauté" mode; add oil and heat it.
2. Add onion, stir, and sauté for 2 minutes.
3. Add turnips, carrots, cumin, and lemon juice, stir and cook for 1 minute.
4. Add salt, pepper, and water, then stir well. Close the lid and cook at high for 6 minutes.
5. Quickly release the pressure, open the air fryer oven lid, and divide turnips and carrots among plates and serve.

Nutrition: Calories: 170 Fat: 9 g Protein: 1 g Sugar: 5 g Carbs: 19 g Fiber: 7 g Sodium: 475 mg

104. Roasted Potatoes

Preparation Time: 16 min   **Cooking Time:** 17 min   **Servings:** 4

Ingredients:

- 2 lb. baby potatoes
- 5 tbsp. vegetable oil
- ½ cup stock
- 1 rosemary spring
- 5 garlic cloves
- Salt and black pepper to taste

Directions:

1. Set your air fryer oven on "Sauté" mode; add oil and heat it.
2. Add potatoes, rosemary and garlic, stir and brown them for 10 minutes.
3. Prick each potato with a knife, add the stock, salt, and pepper to the pot, seal the air fryer oven lid and cook at high for 7 minutes.
4. Quickly release the pressure, open the air fryer oven lid, divide potatoes among plates and serve.

Nutrition: Calories: 250 Fat: 15 g Protein: 2 g Sugar: 1 g

CHAPTER 10:
Dessert

105. Cheesecake Bites

Preparation Time: 40 min   **Cooking Time:** 9 min   **Servings:** 4

Ingredients:

- ½ cup almond flour
- ½ cup and 2 tbsp. erythritol sweetener, divided
- 4 oz. cream cheese, reduced-fat, softened
- ½ tsp. vanilla extract, unsweetened
- 2 tbsp. heavy cream, reduced-fat, divided

Directions:

1. Prepare the cheesecake mixture and for this, place softened cream cheese in a bowl, add cream, vanilla, and ½ cup sweetener and whisk using an electric mixer until smooth.
2. Scoop the mixture on a baking sheet lined with a parchment sheet, then place it in the freezer for 30 minutes until firm.
3. Place flour in a small bowl and stir in the remaining sweetener.
4. Then switch on the air fryer, insert the fryer basket, grease it with olive oil, then shut with its lid, set the fryer at 350°F, and preheat for 5 minutes.
5. Meanwhile, cut the cheesecake mix into bite-size pieces and then coat it with almond flour mixture.
6. Open the fryer, add cheesecake bites in it, close with its lid and cook for 2 minutes until nicely golden and crispy.
7. Serve straight away.

Nutrition: Calories: 198 Cal Carbs: 6 g Fat: 18 g Protein: 3 g Fiber: 0 g

106. Coconut Pie

Preparation Time: 5 min   **Cooking Time:** 45 min   **Servings:** 6

Ingredients:

- ½ cup coconut flour
- ½ cup erythritol sweetener
- 1 cup shredded coconut, unsweetened, divided
- ¼ cup butter, unsalted
- 1 ½ tsp. vanilla extract, unsweetened
- eggs, pastured
- 1 ½ cups milk, low-fat, unsweetened
- ¼ cup shredded coconut, toasted

Directions:

1. Switch on the air fryer, insert fryer basket, grease it with olive oil, then shut with its lid, set the fryer at 350°F, and preheat for 5 minutes.
2. Meanwhile, place all the ingredients in a bowl and whisk until well blended and smooth batter comes together.
3. Take a 6-inches pie pan, grease its oil, then pour in the prepared batter and smooth the top.
4. Open the fryer, place the pie pan in it, close with its lid, and cook for 45 minutes until pie has set and inserted a toothpick into the pie slide out clean.
5. When the air fryer beeps, open its lid, take out the pie pan and let it cool.
6. Garnish the pie with toasted coconut, then cut into slices and serve.

Nutrition: Calories: 236 Cal Carbs: 16 g Fat: 16 g Protein: 3 g Fiber: 2 g

107. Crustless Cheesecake

Preparation Time: 5 min   **Cooking Time:** 10 min   **Servings:** 2

Ingredients:

- 16 oz. cream cheese, reduced-fat, softened
- 2 tbsp. sour cream, reduced-fat
- ¾ cup erythritol sweetener
- 1 tsp. vanilla extract, unsweetened
- 2 eggs, pastured
- ½ tsp. lemon juice

Directions:

1. Switch on the air fryer, insert fryer basket, grease it with olive oil, then shut with its lid, set the fryer at 350°F, and preheat for 5 minutes.
2. Meanwhile, take two 4 inches of springform pans, grease them with oil, and set them aside.
3. Crack the eggs in a bowl and then whisk in lemon juice, sweetener and vanilla until smooth.
4. Whisk in cream cheese and sour cream until blended and then divide the mixture evenly between prepared pans.
5. Open the fryer, place pans in it, close with its lid, and cook for 10 minutes until cakes are set and inserted skewer into the cakes slide out clean.
6. When the air fryer beeps, open its lid, take out the cake pans and let cakes cool in them.
7. Take out the cakes, refrigerate for 3 hours until cooled, and then serve.

Nutrition: Calories: 318 Cal Carbs: 1 g Fat: 29.7 g Protein: 11.7 g Fiber: 0 g

108. Chocolate Lava Cake

Preparation Time: 5 min   **Cooking Time:** 13 min   **Servings:** 2

Ingredients:

- 1 tbsp. flax meal
- ½ tsp. baking powder
- 1 tbsp. cocoa powder, unsweetened
- ½ tbsp. erythritol sweetener
- ⅛ tsp. Stevia sweetener
- ⅛ tsp. vanilla extract, unsweetened
- 1 tbsp. olive oil
- 2 tbsp. water
- 1 egg, pastured

Directions:

1. Switch on the air fryer, insert fryer basket, grease it with olive oil, then shut with its lid, set the fryer at 350°F, and preheat for 5 minutes.
2. Meanwhile, take two cups of the ramekin, grease it with oil, and set it aside.
3. Place all the ingredients in a bowl, whisk until well combined and incorporated, and pour the batter into the ramekin.
4. Open the fryer, place ramekin in it, close with its lid, and cook for 8 minutes until cake is done and inserted skewer into the cake slides out clean.
5. When the air fryer beeps, open its lid, take out the ramekin and let the cake cool in it.
6. Then take out the cake, cut it into slices, and serve.

Nutrition: Calories: 362.8 Cal Carbs: 3.4 g Fat: 33.6 g Protein: 11.7 g Fiber: 0.6 g

109. Vanilla Bread Pudding

Preparation Time: 10 min   **Cooking Time:** 15 min   **Servings:** 4

Ingredients:

- 3 eggs, lightly beaten
- 1 tsp. coconut oil
- 1 tsp. vanilla
- 4 cup bread cube
- ½ tsp. cinnamon
- ¼ cup raisins
- ¼ cup chocolate chips
- 2 cup milk
- ¼ tsp. salt

Directions:

1. Add water into the instant pot, then place the trivet into the pot.
2. Add bread cubes to a baking dish.
3. In a large bowl, mix the remaining ingredients.
4. Pour the bowl mixture into the baking dish on top of bread cubes and cover the dish with foil.
5. Place baking dish on top of the trivet.
6. Seal the pot with the lid and cook on steam mode for 15 minutes.
7. Once done, allow to release pressure naturally, then open the lid.
8. Carefully remove the baking dish from the pot.
9. Serve and enjoy.

Nutrition: Calories: 230 Fat:10.1 g Carbohydrates: 25 g Sugar: 16.7 g Protein: 9.2 g Cholesterol: 135 mg

110. Blueberry Cupcakes

Preparation Time: 10 min   **Cooking Time:** 25 min   **Servings:** 6

Ingredients:

- 2 eggs, lightly beaten
- ¼ cup butter, softened
- ½ tsp. baking soda
- 1 tsp. baking powder
- 1 tsp. vanilla extract
- ½ fresh lemon juice
- 1 lemon zest
- ¼ cup sour cream
- ¼ cup milk
- 1 cup sugar
- ¾ cup fresh blueberries
- 1 cup all-purpose flour
- ¼ tsp. salt

Directions:

1. Add all ingredients into the large bowl and mix well.
2. Empty 1 cup of water into the instant pot, then place trivet into the pot.
3. Pour batter into the silicone cupcake mound and place it on top of the trivet.
4. Seal the pot with the lid and cook on manual high pressure for 25 minutes.
5. Once done, allow to release pressure naturally, then open the lid.
6. Serve and enjoy.

Nutrition: Calories: 330 Fat: 11.6 g Carbohydrates: 53.6 g Sugar: 36 g Protein: 4.9 g Cholesterol: 80 mg

111. Saffron Rice Pudding

Preparation Time: 10 min   **Cooking Time:** 10 min   **Servings:** 6

Ingredients:

- ½ cup rice
- ½ tsp. cardamom powder
- 3 tbsp. almonds, chopped
- 3 tbsp. walnuts, chopped
- 4 cups milk
- ½ cup sugar
- 2 tbsp. shredded coconut
- 1 tsp. saffron
- 3 tbsp. raisins
- 1 tbsp. ghee
- ⅛ tsp. salt
- ½ water

Directions:

1. Add ghee into the pot and set the pot on sauté mode.
2. Add rice and cook for 30 seconds.
3. Add 3 cups milk, coconut, raisins, saffron, nuts, cardamom powder, sugar, ½ cup water, and salt, and blend well.
4. Close the pot with a lid and cook on manual high pressure for 10 minutes.
5. Once done, release pressure naturally for 15 minutes and then release it using the quick-release method. Open the lid.
6. Add remaining milk and stir well; cook on sauté mode for 2 minutes.
7. Serve and enjoy.

Nutrition: Calories: 280 Fat: 9.9 g Carbohydrates: 42.1 g Sugar: 27 g Protein: 8.2 g Cholesterol: 19 mg

---

112. Cardamom Zucchini Pudding

Preparation Time: 10 min   **Cooking Time:** 10 min   **Servings:** 4

Ingredients:

- 1 ¾ cups zucchini, shredded
- 5 oz. half and half
- 5 ½ oz. milk
- 1 tsp. cardamom powder
- ⅓ cup sugar

Directions:

1. Add all ingredients except cardamom into the instant pot and blend well.
2. Close the pot with a lid and cook on manual high pressure for 10 minutes.
3. As soon as done, discharge pressure naturally for 10 minutes and then release it using the quick-release method. Open the lid.
4. Stir in cardamom and serve.

Nutrition: Calories: 138 Fat: 5 g Carbohydrates: 22.1 g Sugar: 19.4 g Protein: 3 g Cholesterol: 16 mg

113. Yummy Strawberry Cobbler

Preparation Time: 10 min   **Cooking Time:** 12 min   **Servings:** 3

Ingredients:

- 1 cup strawberries, sliced
- ½ tsp. vanilla
- ⅓ cup butter
- 1 cup milk
- 1 tsp. baking powder
- ½ cup granulated sugar
- 1 ¼ cup all-purpose flour

Directions:

1. In a huge container, add all ingredients except strawberries and stir to combine.
2. Add sliced strawberries and fold well.
3. Grease ramekins with cooking spray, then pour batter into the ramekins.
4. Discharge 1 ½ cups water into the instant pot, then place the trivet in the pot.
5. Place ramekins on top of the trivet.
6. Close the pot with a lid and cook on manual high pressure for 12 minutes.
7. As soon as done, discharge pressure naturally for 10 minutes and then release it using the quick-release method. Open the lid.
8. Serve and enjoy.

Nutrition: Calories: 555 Fat: 22.8 g Carbohydrates: 81.7 g Sugar: 39.6 g Protein: 8.6 g Cholesterol: 61 mg

---

114. Peach Cobbler

Preparation Time: 10 min   **Cooking Time:** 20 min   **Servings:** 6

Ingredients:

- 20 oz. can peach pie filling
- 1 ½ tsp. cinnamon
- ¼ tsp. nutmeg
- 14 ½ oz. vanilla cake mix
- ½ cup butter, melted

Directions:

1. Add peach pie filling into the instant pot.
2. In a bulky container, mix the remaining ingredients and spread them over peach pie filling.
3. Close the pot with a lid and cook on manual high pressure for 10 minutes.
4. As soon as done, discharge pressure naturally for 10 minutes and then release it using the quick-release method. Open the lid.
5. Serve and enjoy.

Nutrition: Calories: 445 Fat: 15.4 g Carbohydrates: 76.1 g Sugar: 47.7 g Protein: 0.2 g Cholesterol: 41 mg

115. Apple Pear Crisp

Preparation Time: 10 min   **Cooking Time:** 20 min   **Servings:** 4

Ingredients:
- 4 apples, peel, and cut into chunks
- 1 cup steel-cut oats
- 2 pears, cut into chunks
- 1 ½ cup water
- ½ tsp. cinnamon
- ¼ cup maple syrup

Directions:
1. Add all ingredients into the instant pot and stir well.
2. Seal the pot with a lid and cook on manual high for 10 minutes.
3. As soon as done, reduce pressure naturally for 10 minutes and then release it using the quick-release method. Open the lid.
4. Serve warm and enjoy.

Nutrition: Calories: 306 Fat: 1.9 g Carbohydrates: 74 g Sugar: 45.3 g Protein: 3.7 g Cholesterol:

116. Vanilla Peanut Butter Fudge

Preparation Time: 10 min   **Cooking Time:** 90 min   **Servings:** 12

Ingredients:
- 1 cup chocolate chips
- 8 ½ oz. cream cheese
- ¼ cup peanut butter
- ½ tsp. vanilla
- ¼ cup swerve

Directions:
1. Add all ingredients into the instant pot and stir well.
2. Seal the pot with a lid and cook on slow cook mode for 60 minutes.
3. Once done, release pressure using the quick-release method, then open the lid.
4. Stir until smooth and cook for 30 minutes more on sauté mode.
5. Pour mixture into the baking pan and place in the fridge until set.
6. Slice and serve.

Nutrition: Calories: 177 Fat: 13.9 g Carbohydrates: 14.9 g Sugar: 12.8 g Protein: 3.9 g Cholesterol: 25 mg

30 Day Meal Plan

There are many possibilities of combining foods that allow you to have up to 1000 different feeding days

Days	Breakfast	Lunch	Dinner	Dessert
1	HAM AND CHEESE ENGLISH MUFFIN MELT	CHICKEN COCONUT POPPERS	MOIST & JUICY BAKED COD	CHEESECAKE BITES
2	AIR FRYER BACON	SPINACH BEER HEART	BAGEL CRUST FISH FILLETS	COCONUT PIE
3	PUMPKIN PIE FRENCH TOAST	EASY AIR FRYER SCALLOPS	STRAWBERRIES OATMEAL	CRUSTLESS CHEESECAKE

4	BREAKFAST CHEESE BREAD CUPS	**ROSEMARY LAMB CHOPS**	BEEF-CHICKEN MEATBALL CASSEROLE	CHOCOLATE LAVA CAKE
5	GRILLED CHEESE SANDWICHES	PAPRIKA PULLED PORK	DIET BOILED RIBS	SAFFRON RICE PUDDING
6	AIR FRIED EGGS	PARMESAN BEEF SUCES	EASY AIR FRYER SCALLOPS	YUMMY STRAWBERRY COBBLER
7	MUSHROOM AND CHEESE FRITTATA	CHICKEN COCONUT POPPERS	SCRAMBLED EGGS	PEACH COBBLER
8	CRISPY BREAKFAST AVOCADO FRIES	SPINACH BEER HEART	MOIST & JUICY BAKED COD	CHOCOLATE LAVA CAKE
9	CHEESE AND EGG BREAKFAST SANDWICH	BEEF-CHICKEN MEATBALL CASSEROLE	BAGEL CRUST FISH FILLETS	APPLE PEAR CRISP
10	HAM AND CHEESE ENGLISH MUFFIN MELT	AIR FRYER PORK RIBS	ITALIAN WHOLE CHICKEN	VANILLA BREAD PUDDING
11	PEANUT BUTTER AND BANANA BREAKFAST SANDWICH	GARLIC BEEF STEAK	STRAWBERRIES OATMEAL	BLUEBERRY CUPCAKES
12	GRILLED CHEESE SANDWICHES	PAPRIKA PULLED PORK	SPINACH BEER HEART	SAFFRON RICE PUDDING
13	PUMPKIN PIE FRENCH TOAST	BAGEL CRUST FISH FILLETS	PARMESAN BEEF SUCES	CHOCOLATE LAVA CAKE
14	AIR FRYER BACON	BEEF-CHICKEN MEATBALL CASSEROLE	EASY AIR FRYER SCALLOPS	CHEESECAKE BITES
15	AVOCADO AND BLUEBERRY MUFFINS	MOIST & JUICY BAKED COD	CHICKEN COCONUT POPPERS	COCONUT PIE
16	AIR FRIED EGGS	SCRAMBLED EGGS	PAPRIKA PULLED PORK	YUMMY STRAWBERRY COBBLER
17	MUSHROOM AND CHEESE FRITTATA	CRISPY FISH STICKS IN AIR FRYER	SPINACH BEER HEART	APPLE PEAR CRISP
18	BREAKFAST CHEESE BREAD CUPS	CHICKEN COCONUT POPPERS	MOIST & JUICY BAKED COD	PEACH COBBLER

19	HAM AND CHEESE ENGLISH MUFFIN MELT	STRAWBERRIES OATMEAL	PARMESAN BEEF SUCES	CRUSTLESS CHEESECAKE
20	GRILLED CHEESE SANDWICHES	AIR FRYER PORK RIBS	BEEF-CHICKEN MEATBALL CASSEROLE	BLUEBERRY CUPCAKES
21	AIR FRYER BACON	EASY AIR FRYER SCALLOPS	PARMESAN BEEF SUCES	SAFFRON RICE PUDDING
22	CRISPY BREAKFAST AVOCADO FRIES	STRAWBERRIES OATMEAL	BAGEL CRUST FISH FILLETS	YUMMY STRAWBERRY COBBLER
23	PEANUT BUTTER AND BANANA BREAKFAST SANDWICH	PAPRIKA PULLED PORK	MOIST & JUICY BAKED COD	PEANUT BUTTER FUDGE
24	PUMPKIN PIE FRENCH TOAST	GARLIC BEEF STEAK	SCRAMBLED EGGS	PEACH COBBLER
25	BREAKFAST CHEESE BREAD CUPS	CHICKEN COCONUT POPPERS	SPINACH BEER HEART	CHEESECAKE BITES
26	PUMPKIN PIE FRENCH TOAST	PAPRIKA PULLED PORK	STRAWBERRIES OATMEAL	BLUEBERRY CUPCAKES
27	AVOCADO AND BLUEBERRY MUFFINS	SPINACH BEER HEART	EASY AIR FRYER SCALLOPS	APPLE PEAR CRISP
28	HAM AND CHEESE ENGLISH MUFFIN MELT	MOIST & JUICY BAKED COD	BAGEL CRUST FISH FILLETS	SAFFRON RICE PUDDING
29	AIR FRIED EGGS	PARMESAN BEEF SUCES	AIR FRYER PORK RIBS	COCONUT PIE
30	MUSHROOM AND CHEESE FRITTATA	EASY AIR FRYER SCALLOPS	CHICKEN COCONUT POPPERS	CRUSTLESS CHEESECAKE

Conclusion

Diabetes is a type of condition in which the blood sugar or glucose levels are abnormally high. Glucose is produced by the food you eat. Insulin is a hormone that allows glucose to enter cells and provide them with energy. Insulin is not produced by your body if you have type 1 diabetes. Type 2 diabetes is a more severe form of diabetes in which your body does not manufacture or use insulin properly. In Prediabetes, glucose stays in the blood due to a lack of insulin. This suggests that blood sugar levels are higher than typical but not high enough to be classified as diabetic. People that have prediabetes are more likely to develop type 2 diabetes.

Over time, having too much glucose in the blood will cause serious problems. Your brain, kidneys, and nerves may be affected. Diabetes can lead to heart failure, stroke, and possibly the need to amputate a limb. Pregnant women can also develop diabetes, which is known as gestational diabetes. Using the Air Fryer is a smart way to help your diabetes control and reduce the disease's effects.

Air frying uses less fat than conventional frying, making it a great way to reduce calories and fat in your diet. It is also an easy way to cook meals that are healthier and tasted better than ever.

Diabetic people are known to live longer lives than non-diabetics. While this is not a surefire indicator of their health, it shows that blood sugar level control is of great importance. Research has shown that food cooked in an air fryer is healthier and better for controlling blood sugar levels than other cooking types.

You need to cook well to control blood sugar levels effectively as a person with diabetes. This means that you need to incorporate low on carbs and high protein into your diet. The air fryer is the ideal appliance as it cooks food safely and healthily.

Imagine eating delicious food without all the fat and calories. That's the promise of air frying. You wouldn't know you were eating.

Air frying is a healthy alternative to conventional cooking that is quickly becoming a favorite among people with diabetes and who care about their weight. It also presents an opportunity for those who do not have diabetes to enjoy healthier meals without giving up tasty foods.

There are many benefits to a diet based on blood sugar levels. Doctors and nurses recommend that people with diabetes eat high protein foods to help regulate their blood sugar. Air fryers can produce foods that mimic this type of food to get the same benefits as if they were eating the food normally. It is easier to prepare and requires less fat to cook these foods. This is why air frying is becoming more popular among diabetics and non-diabetics alike.

Hence, by eating healthy food, being physically active will keep your glucose level in check and make sure your body does not become overweight or obese. The most really important thing you can do is make sure the quality of your lifestyle is healthy, which majorly consists of you being conscious of what you eat and how much you are willing to follow the rules. There are many ways to live a healthy life, including keeping track of your sugar level. Lower your diabetes chances, make sure your glucose level is under control, or not experience pre-diabetic symptoms. But, if you already have developed diabetes, you need to increase the effort to live a healthy, balanced life.

Therefore, we want you to live a healthy life without missing out on life or delicious foods. Now, you can eat fried foods with an air fryer. Air fryer cuts back the need to use oil hence, cutting back on calories and bad cholesterol. Furthermore, it increases the quality of the food. All the food is prepared in front of your eyes. Added preservatives or too many spices and salt do not go in the recipes. You can enjoy the best of both worlds.

In a nutshell, using an air fryer for healthy living is nothing short of a surprise. You can still eat your favorite fried foods, with fewer calories and more added flavors, and even live a healthy, balanced life and minimize your risk of Obesity, Diabetes, and other diseases.

Printed in Great Britain
by Amazon

19576960R00054